W9-CMP-670

371.33
Ham

ISSUES **THAT CONCERN YOU**

Electronic Devices in Schools

Jill Hamilton, *Book Editor*

Christine Nasso, *Publisher*
Elizabeth Des Chenes, *Managing Editor*

GREENHAVEN PRESS
A part of Gale, Cengage Learning

GALE
CENGAGE Learning

Detroit • New York • San Francisco • New Haven, Conn • Waterville, Maine • London

LIBRARY OF CONGRESS CATALOGING-IN-PUBLICATION DATA
Electronic devices in schools / Jill Hamilton, book editor.
p. cm. — (Issues that concern you)
Includes bibliographical references and index.
ISBN-13: 978-0-7377-3985-5 (hardcover)
1. Educational technology—United States. 2. Education—Effect of technological innovations on—United States. 3. Mobile communication systems—United States. 4. Laptop computers—United States. 5. Classroom management—United States. I. Hamilton, Jill.
LB1028.3.E427 2007
371.33—dc22
2007036331

ISBN-10: 0-7377-3985-1

Printed in the United States of America
5 6 7 12 11 10

CONTENTS

School policies surrounding electronic devices in schools can be contentious. Although in past decades minor skirmishes occurred between students' and school faculty members over students bringing calculators to class, and later, pagers and beepers, recent advances in electronic technology have created a host of new issues and questions. Looking only at changes in cell phones provides insight into some of the challenges facing administrators, parents, and students.

With the earliest cell phones the issues seemed relatively clear-cut to school officials. Cell phones were disruptive and, therefore, not generally allowed in class. Cells phones were not nearly as ubiquitous as they are now, and were larger in size, so they were easier for school administrators to ban from the classrooms and made it easier to enforce that ban.

As cell phones have become more advanced, school administrators are finding themselves facing a variety of unfamiliar issues. New features create unforeseen problems. Cell phones are not being used only to make or receive calls but also to send text messages, provide Web access, and take pictures and video. Additionally, the ever-changing functions of phones make it difficult to create clear-cut guidelines. For example, if cell phones are allowed but handheld computers are banned, what should the rule be for cell phones with Internet access?

A primary concern of many school administrators is that cell phones will be used for cheating. Students could use a well-equipped cell phone, for example, to take a picture of a test and then distribute it within minutes to their circle of friends. They could also text the answers to someone else or send out a request for help. A student could also store information, such as chemistry formulas, in the phone. Or a stumped student could even look up an answer online.

Administrators also have concerns about privacy, and cell phones with camera and video capability raise many privacy issues. In addition to photographing tests, such devices can also be used for locker-room snooping, mocking other people, and embarrassing teachers. The video-sharing site YouTube is filled with videos of teachers behaving badly, and "moblogs," mobile Web logs, can be used to post pictures mocking other students.

Students and parents in some states, however, feel that the positive attributes of cell phones far outweigh the risk of cheating or the possibility of inappropriate use. After seeing how cell phones were used during the Columbine shootings and the September 11 terrorist attacks, many now view cell phones as a necessary safety device. These parents and students argue that administrators need to combat cheating and inappropriate behaviors in ways that do not involve outright cell phone bans.

When school administrators have tried to ban cell phones from schools, they have often met with obstacles. The most contentious

In the twenty-first century, cell phones and other portable electronic devices have become a common sight in American schools.

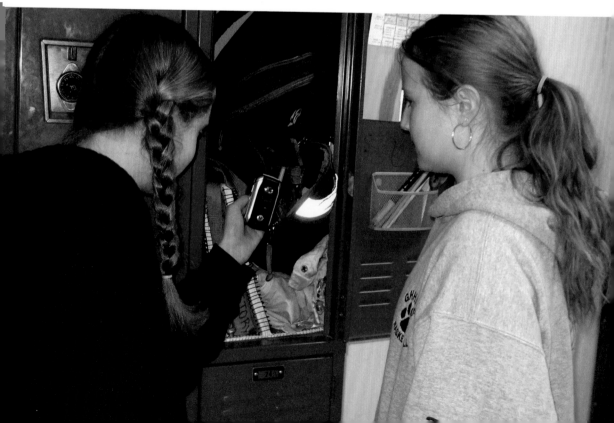

fight over a ban on electronic devices in schools has been in New York City. In 2006 Mayor Michael Bloomberg started aggressively enforcing the ban by subjecting students to random searches with metal detectors. This angered many parents who felt that their children needed cell phones for emergencies. The parents reacted by writing angry letters, holding rallies and news conferences, and filing lawsuits. Students showed their displeasure in more subversive ways, such as smuggling their phones into school in lunches or hiding the phones in their pants where they know they will not be patted down. As this book went to press, the issue remained contentious and had not reached a satisfactory resolution.

Although the New York City case shows that many parents and students see cell phones as a necessary safety device, others have argued that cell phones actually make schools less safe. Students have caused safety problems by calling in bomb threats from untraceable cell phones. And many safety experts argue that, in an emergency, panicked students using cell phones will create confusion, jam phone lines, and aid the spread of false information.

As cell phones continue to evolve, the rules for them will need to evolve as well. As such technology becomes more a part of daily life, schools will continually need to reexamine and adjust school policies. Issues such as cheating and inappropriate use will inevitably be balanced with student rights and safety issues.

Cell phones in schools is just one of the issues related to electronic devices that teachers, parents, and administrators are facing today. Authors in this anthology debate the merits of laptops in classrooms and the use of PDAs, among other topics. In addition, there are several appendixes for the readers who are interested in further exploring the topic. "What You Should Know About Electronic Devices in Schools" gives readers a quick, bulleted look at pertinent facts about the issues. "What You Should Do About Electronic Devices in Schools" offers concrete suggestions for those who would like to take action. The appendixes also include an extensive bibliography of media sources and a list of organizations to contact. *Issues That Concern You: Electronic Devices in Schools* offers a wide-ranging look at the current issues surrounding this continually evolving topic.

ONE

Schools Struggle with Rules for Electronic Devices

Ellen R. DeLisio

> The following selection from *Education World*, a publica-
> tion for educators, offers an overview of some of the issues
> that school administrators face as students bring in cell
> phones with texting, Internet, and video capabilities. At
> first, when the technology was new, schools simply banned
> cell phones on campus. But they have had to recraft their
> policies as new issues develop. One big change came in the
> wake of the 9/11 and Columbine tragedies when parents
> started viewing cell phones as a safety necessity for their
> children. Phones with camera and video capabilities have
> also raised new concerns, such as whether they should be
> allowed in private places such as locker rooms or even be
> allowed on campus at all. DeLisio is the editor of news and
> features for *Education World*.

Just a few years ago, it looked like regulating cellular phone use
in schools was getting a lot easier. Cell phones had become
ubiquitous and innocuous, and making it a school offense or even
a crime to possess them on school grounds didn't make much sense
anymore.

But just as states and school districts were relaxing their policies, along came a new generation of cell phone—with cameras,

Internet access, and text messaging—that it seems every teen must have. Now administrators are wrestling with how to permit the legitimate use of phones, while preventing possible privacy violations and cheating.

The Evolution of Technology

"Cell phones still are an issue, but not the same issue," said Dr. William Scharffe, president of the American Association of Policy Services, a work-alike group with the National School Boards Association (NSBA), and director of bylaw and policy services for the Michigan Association of School Boards. "The main concern is prohibiting use during instructional time and not disrupting the school atmosphere. . . . As the cell phone industry improved the product, it became more problematic for schools."

When cell phones, pagers, and beepers began to spread into the mainstream in the late 1980s and early 1990s, most districts and even states moved to ban them from school grounds. Beepers and pagers were associated with the drug trade, and it was feared if a student had one or the other, he or she was or wanted to be a drug dealer.

Some of the regulations originally were not written to apply to phones, but many were expanded to cover phones by including electronic devices among the banned items.

New Technology Means New Policies

Technological and social changes and national events . . . though, have prompted a review of policies. Advances in cell phone technology and the explosion of the industry made phones less of a luxury item and more a convenience, particularly for working parents trying to keep track of children. The other influences were more sudden and jarring: the shootings at Columbine High School in April 1999, and the terrorist attacks of September 11, 2001.

People watched and heard as cell phones linked victims and potential victims to their loved ones and the outside world. Parents now wanted to be in closer contact with their children, and argued to school districts that cell phones were necessary for safety.

Still, some school administrators are wary of opening the gate. The New York City Public Schools, the largest district in the U.S., and one most affected by the terrorist attacks, still forbids students to have any electronic devices in their possession. But school officials are reviewing the policy, and may revise it to allow students to carry cell phones, as long as the devices are turned off during the school day, said Marge Feinberg, a spokeswoman for the district.

"One reason we are looking at the policy is because of 9/11," Feinberg said. "Some cell phones still were able to operate that day."

But in most places, change has come.

"We have gotten a lot of information about major changes and school districts looking at policies," according to Naomi Gittins, staff attorney for the NSBA. "Many states are repealing the laws [regulating cell phones in schools] and are throwing the issue back at the local districts."

Rules Made at the Local Level

That is the case in Connecticut, whose state legislature revised its law regulating cell phone possession in schools to give local districts more latitude in dealing with the issue, said Vincent Mustaro, senior staff associate for policy for the Connecticut Association of Boards of Education (CABE).

"School officials around the U.S. began to say that an outright ban was not realistic," Mustaro told *Education World*. "Parents are encouraging kids to carry phones. One school principal estimated that 70 percent of the kids in his school had phones. I think the change is connected to school violence and a desire by parents to be more in touch with their kids, and the popularity and availability of phones continues to grow."

"There are more important things we want administrators involved in," than policing cell phone possession, Mustaro added.

At the same time, CABE is making it clear to school districts that cell phones should not be visible or used during instructional time.

New York City Councilmen Robert Jackson (center), Charles Barron, and Letitia James speak with reporters. They are responding to a petition by thousands of New York City parents that protests the ban on cell phones in schools.

"The position we take is that cell phones don't belong in classroom settings unless there is a specific reason, such as a medical disability that requires students to be in touch with a parent," he said. "They are a disruption and shouldn't be on during instructional time. They are not allowed in classrooms, and if they are there, they are confiscated."

CABE also recommends that camera phones be banned from schools because they can be secretly used to take pictures of people and violate privacy and be used for cheating, he said.

Dr. Scharffe said he recommends similar policies to schools in Michigan. "I advise them that they can allow phones if they wish, but to limit their use; there should be no use during instructional time, they are a disruption to instruction and the school atmosphere. Most schools are not going to make a big deal about it. You can bring the phone to school, but you can't use it."

He also suggests banning camera phones or ones that can send text messages, even if students or parents argue that those are the only type of phone a student has. "If safety is the issue [for owning a phone], just give students phones that make and receive calls," Dr. Scharffe said. "Most schools ban camera phones and those with Internet connections."

As for whether screening for different types of student phones could create more headaches for administrators, Dr. Scharffe said once the policy is clear, students have to live with the consequences. "If they use [camera phones], they lose them," he said. "If they bring camera phones to school, someone will talk, and it will be discovered."

The National Association of Secondary School Principals (NASSP) agrees that districts and schools should decide the policies, said spokesman Michael Carr.

"From our perspective, it is better left up to the local level to set policies," Carr told *Education World*. "It's not as much an issue of calling now as it is cameras and text messaging. We hear some talk among members about trying to make it work—balancing the priorities."

Studies Can Influence Policies

Middleburg High School in Middleburg, Florida, has seen its cell phone policy change twice in three years as the state laws eased. Up until recently, state law required disciplinary action if a student had a wireless communication device on school grounds.

Middleburg students had a hand in changing the law [in 2004], researching the state law and then urging legislators to change the regulations. Now the state allows students to possess a wireless communications device while on school property or in attendance at a school function, and it is up to each school board to adopt rules governing the use of wireless communications devices.

Pager and Cell Phone Policies

Statutes Prohibiting Pagers and/or Cellular Phones

State	Object(s) prohibited	Prohibited for whom/where
AL	Pocket pager, electronic communication device	Pupil possession in school
AR	Paging device, beeper, or similar electronic communication device	On school campus
CT	Remotely activated paging device	Pupil use or possession in public school
IL	Pocket pager or similar electronic paging device	Student possession or use while in any school building or on any school property at any time
LA	Electronic communication device, "including any facsimile system, radio paging service, mobile telephone service, intercom or electromechanical paging system"	Effective beginning with the 2003–2004 school year, student use in any public elementary or secondary school or on the grounds thereof or in a school bus used to transport public school students
MI	Pocket pager, electronic communication device or other personal communication device	Students in school
NJ	Remotely activated paging device	K–12 student to bring or possess at any time on school property
PA	Beepers	Student possession "on school grounds, at school-sponsored activities and on buses or other vehicles provided by the school district"
RI	Paging device of any kind	K–12 student while on school property
WI	Electronic paging or two-way communication device	Student possession or use on school property

As of the [2004–2005] school year, Middleburg students are allowed to carry cell phones, but they must be off at all times. If a student is found using a phone during the school day, the punishment is an automatic three-day, out-of-school suspension, principal Dr. David McDonald said. The school does not prohibit camera phones or those that can send text messages.

[As recently as 2002], a student could receive a ten-day suspension for having a phone in school, although the length of the suspension could be reduced at the discretion of the principal, Dr. McDonald told *Education World*. [In 2004], that policy allowed students to bring cell phones to school, but they had to be turned off and in lockers. If a student was found carrying one, the penalty was a three-day in-school suspension. If they had one and it rang, it was a three-day out-of-school suspension.

"We realized that kids needed them after school," said McDonald, adding that most of the 1,700 students in his school have cell phones.

The technology changes and the overwhelming number of student cell phones at St. Elizabeth High School in Wilmington, Delaware, prompted school officials to revise the cell phone policy for [the] school year, said John Forester, the school's dean of students.

"It seems like every student has one," Forester told *Education World*. "Probably 90 percent of the 420 high school students have phones."

No Cameras in Locker Rooms or Texting in Class

A problem school officials have encountered is students, mostly girls, according to Forester, secretly sending text messages to friends in other schools during class.

The new policy requires that phones be shut off, but students can carry their phones in their lockers, purses, or pockets. If students use a phone during the school day or if one rings during class, the student receives demerits. Camera phones are not forbidden, but the policy states that no cell phone photographs are allowed in the locker rooms or restrooms.

"We haven't heard many complaints," Forester said. "If a parent calls a phone while a student is in class, the student still gets a demerit, and the phone is confiscated for the day. The biggest offense is a phone ringing in class—and it's usually a parent."

Balancing Needs of Students and Officials

Now administrators are bracing for the ramifications of increased cell phone access, even as the technology continues to evolve and reaches younger students.

"Now the issue extends down to the elementary grades," Dr. Scharffe said. "There are first and second graders with cell phones. School districts across the land never thought they would have to deal with elementary students with cell phones."

Law enforcement officials also disagree on the benefits of students having cell phones, Dr. Scharffe added. "It would jam the system if [during an emergency] 250 people tried to call out from a school at one time," he said. "During the siege at Columbine, there were so many cell phone calls going out from the school that it clogged the system." Sheriff's departments in some communities have addressed the safety issue by providing students with pre-programmed cell phones that only can be used to dial 911 and cannot receive calls, Dr. Scharffe noted.

Schools also could lose some control in emergencies, according to Dr. McDonald. "I think this is creating a situation where we all have to deal with things differently," he said. "In the past, we could manage information in an emergency situation. But if students have phones, they will find a way to use them. There could be a lot of misinformation going out there."

Careful monitoring of policies and phone use are solid approaches for most administrators, researchers agreed. "The best you can do is set reasonable policies," Dr. Scharffe added.

TWO

Electronic Devices Should Be Required, Not Banned

Mike Elgan

Mike Elgan argues that banning iPods and other electronic devices will not prepare students for life in the modern world. "Kids should learn how to efficiently pack a gadget or computer full of content and figure out how to quickly access and use that content to solve problems and answer questions," he writes. Students who successfully use iPods to retrieve information are not cheating, he argues, but learning to gather data in a quick and efficient manner. He points out that, in a world in which information is easily available to anyone, the rote memorization taught in schools is no longer a useful skill. Elgan is a technology writer and the former editor of *Windows* magazine.

The Associated Press published an article . . . about high schools increasingly banning iPods because some kids use them to cheat.

The article, reprinted in *USA Today* and hundreds of other newspapers, reported one example where a school "recently enacted a ban on digital media players after school officials realized some students were downloading formulas and other material onto the players."

Mike Elgan, "Are iPod-Banning Schools Cheating Our Kids?" *www.computerworld.com*, May 4, 2007. Copyright © 2007 Computerworld Inc. All rights reserved. Reproduced by permission.

I don't want to second-guess the individual decisions of specific teachers and school principals. But the ban does raise questions, the most interesting of which is: Should iPods or other handheld gadgets instead be "required" during tests?

What the iPod Ban Teaches Kids

Most high school students prepare for tests by guessing what facts might be on the test, then trying to memorize those facts

Nick d'Ambrosia holds up his iPod inside a classroom at his school, Mountain View High in Meridian, Idaho. The district recently banned iPods and similar devices over concerns about cheating.

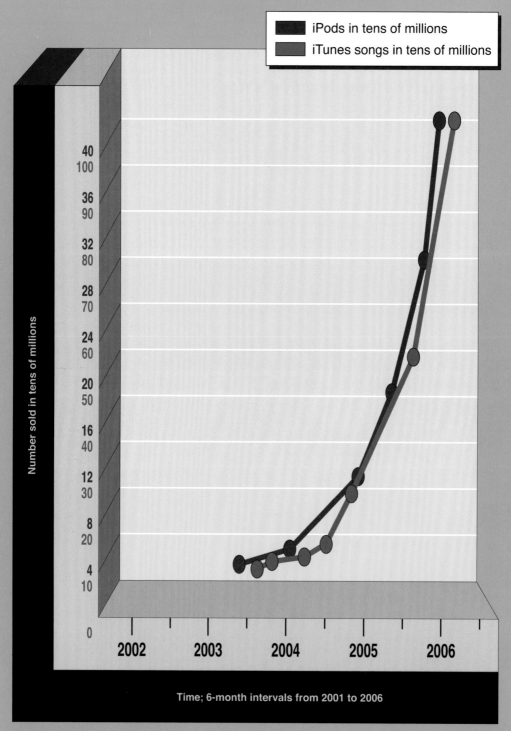

iTunes vs. iPods Sold

iPods in tens of millions
iTunes songs in tens of millions

Number sold in tens of millions

Time; 6-month intervals from 2001 to 2006

Taken from: BizHack

to maximize their grades. Hours after the test, those facts tend to be forgotten. This is a gross oversimplification, sure, but largely true.

How much of your high school history, science or math do you still retain to this day? If you're like me, the answer is practically zero.

In my case, the single most valuable thing I learned in high school was how to touch-type (thank you, Ms. Balish!). Skills, habits and experiences, more than temporarily memorized facts, are what turn us into adults who can learn.

So many college students I've met—even at some of the nation's top universities—are there because they have an aptitude for memorization. Many straight-A high school students have few interests, little curiosity and zero inclination toward intellectual discovery. Our system rewards the memorizers and punishes the creative thinkers.

An iPod, when used during tests, is nothing more than a machine that stores and spits out data. By banning iPods and other gadgets, we're teaching kids to actually become iPods—to become machines that store and spit out data. Instead, we should be teaching them to use iPods—to use that data and to be human beings who can think—and leave data storage to the machines.

By banning iPods, we're preparing our kids for a world without the Internet, a world without iPods, a world without electronic gadgets that can store information. But is that the world they're going to live in?

What iPods Teach Kids

What are those iPod cheaters doing, really? They're creatively putting facts at their fingertips using ubiquitous technology in preparation for using those facts.

Isn't that a more realistic preparation for college, career and life than teaching memorization?

When I go into a meeting, deliver a presentation, write a column or develop a report, electronic gadgets and Internet-connected PCs are always part of the process. My ability to use those devices and my ability to think critically using the universe of facts always at hand determines to a large degree the quality of my work.

Memorizing information is valuable but not as valuable as the ability to find and use information. Yet we teach the low-value skill and ban the valuable one.

When kids take math tests, most teachers require them to "show their work" instead of doing problems "in their heads." Or they require calculators. Teachers are preparing students to function in a world where pencils and calculators are generally available. Banning iPods is like banning pencils or calculators.

What's the point of creating an unrealistic scenario that involves the total absence of widely available tools? Outside the classroom and after high school, a student can "always" have access to an iPod or an Internet-connected phone or computer.

Schools Need to Learn, Too

If Johnny can get an "A" by using his iPod, what does that tell us about the necessity of memorizing the knowledge? What does that tell us about the power of electronic gadgets?

The larger, more interesting question is: Why do we devote so much time and energy teaching kids to memorize facts we know they'll forget? We should instead teach critical thinking, creative decision-making and sophisticated information retrieval.

We should teach kids how to function in the real world—the world they live in, not the world their grandparents lived in.

That means kids should learn how to efficiently pack a gadget or computer full of content and figure out how to quickly access and use that content to solve problems and answer questions.

We need the iPod equivalent of "open-book tests," where gadgets are required, the tests are harder and demand of the student problem solving, creative thinking and deep understanding of the ideas, not just the ability to spit out words fed to them earlier.

Kids need to learn relevant skills in order to function in a changing world. Schools need to learn, too. It's time that schools accept the fact that the Internet and little electronic info-gadgets are everywhere and here to stay.

A revolution has occurred. In one generation, we've transformed a world where information is scarce and hard to find to a world where nearly all knowledge can be available to everyone, all the time.

THREE

Students Should Unplug in Class

Valerie Schultz

One of the rules teacher Valerie Schultz has in her class-room is "Unplug." She disagrees with her students' asser-tions that they can pay attention if they only have one ear-bud connected. She also worries about hearing damage, especially when she can hear a student's bass line from sev-eral feet away. But mostly, she worries that iPods are a way for students to shut out the rest of the world. "Making them unplug every now and then may turn out to improve not only their future ability to hear, but their current connec-tions to their fellow humans," she writes.

It has taken since August [2006], but my high school students now know what to do when they hear this word: "Unplug." I say this when someone has come into class, and he or she has for-gotten to take the iPod earbuds out of his or her ears. Even if the iPod is turned off, I still don't want that wire snaking out of the ears and down into the shirt or the pocket. My students seem to think that they can be attentive to the world around them if one earbud, with the volume turned down low, is nestled in one ear, and the other ear is tuned to real time. Unfortunately, when it comes to paying attention in English class, there is no contest. Music wins every time. Hence one of the classroom rules: "Unplug."

Kids are listening to their iPods 24/7, as they say. No matter how early in the morning or how late at night, even while sound asleep in bed, their iPods are funneling music into their heads. It's as though their lives need a constant soundtrack; as though a moment without background music is a moment not fully *lived*. "My iPod is my *life*," says one of my students, in deadly earnest.

I am too old to understand this mentality. The older I get, the fonder I am of the quiet. Although I suspect my age is more of a state of mind, since my husband enthusiastically bought one of the very-first-generation iPods. He sometimes listens to his iPod in bed, which he says helps him get to sleep long after I am soundly slumbering. Now those first iPods look like enormous, laughable dinosaurs when compared to the tiny sleek latest ones, but of course my husband has upgraded. He is a techno-freak. He is married, however, to a techno-indifferent.

Our daughters all have iPods, in various cute shapes and colors, with varying capacities to hold music. They plug them into their cars and computers like magical things. When they move

Some scientists have blamed the popularity of music players like iPods for hearing loss among young people.

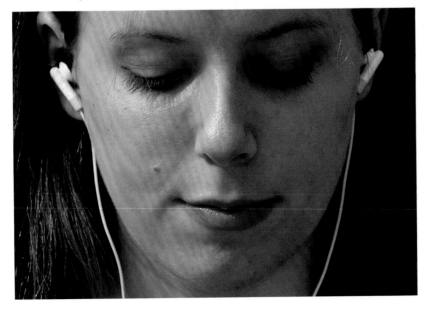

to a new apartment, they do not have to haul huge heavy boxes of albums, like we used to, or even smaller, more manageable collections of CDs. They actually don't have to pack their iPods at all, because they are wearing them, like earrings or a belt. Their music has become as personal as clothing.

Tools for Cheating

In classrooms, iPods have become more than harmless distractions: they have become tools of cheating, much like cell phones or painstakingly tiny writing on the forearm. Apparently some clever but misguided students were downloading answers onto their iPods, and then accessing the information during tests. (Much like prison inmates who ingeniously devise illicit weapons, one wishes the creativity and problem-solving skills apparent in these enterprises were put to some nobler use for the common good.)

Interestingly, I have read the counter-argument that iPods, rather than being banned in classrooms, should be required. Instead of relying on the old, perhaps irrelevant tool of memo-

Recommended Listening Time per Day to Prevent Hearing Loss

% of Volume Control	Earbud	Supra-Aural (headphones that rest on top of the ear)
10–50%	No Limit	No Limit
60%	No Limit	No Limit
70%	6 hours	20 hours
80%	1.5 hours	4.9 hours
90%	22 minutes	1.2 hours
100%	5 minutes	18 minutes

Taken from: National Hearing Conservation Association

rization (after all, how much memorized high school stuff does *anyone* remember?), students should be learning how to take full advantage of the revolution in technology. We should teach them "critical thinking, creative decision-making and sophisticated information retrieval. . . . Let's teach them how to deal with the new problem of too much information," writes Mike Elgan, in an article in the magazine *Computerworld*. Elgan believes that the ban on iPods in high schools is proof that the current educational system "rewards the memorizers and punishes the creative thinkers."

Spoken like a true creative thinker. Or a lousy memorizer.

I do feel that the administrative powers of public schools tend to condemn whatever new trends young people are following prior to making the slightest attempt to understand them. With a little thought and patience, perhaps the adults could more easily incorporate into school life the students' passion for developing technology. If there is one thing high school students could surely use more of, it's passion. For anything.

Dangerous Decibels

On the other hand, I worry that all of my students (and children) will be stone deaf by the time they are 30 if they continue to blast dangerous levels of decibels directly into their ear canals. Hearing loss, after all, accumulates over one's lifetime. According to a report on National Public Radio, "Six years ago, researchers at the Centers for Disease Control and Prevention reported noise-induced hearing loss in nearly 13 percent of Americans between 6 and 19," which translates to a number of roughly 5 million kids whose hearing may be muffled. While the researchers' conclusions are open to debate in the scientific community, they give me pause. Sometimes, when my students enter the classroom, or when one of my daughters is in the backseat, I can hear the bass line of a song through earbuds that are nowhere near my ears. If the sound is leaking out of their heads from several feet away, the volume is definitely too loud to be safe for the poor ears in which the earbuds are blasting. The ringing in the ears that people of my generation remember experiencing after live concerts, and which signifies imminent damage to the ears, is heard on a daily basis by many young iPod devotees. It would be comparable to going to a Grateful Dead concert *every day*.

One of my students told me that she likes being able to tune out the rest of the world through the use of her iPod, as though she floated within a protective bubble of her favorite music. I understand the attraction, but her statement made me feel uneasy. It occurred to me that maybe our teenagers really don't need any more help in shutting people out. Making them unplug every now and then may turn out to improve not only their future ability to hear, but their current connections to their fellow humans.

FOUR

Banning iPods Will Not Stop Student Cheating

Michael Bertacchi

In the following selection Michael Bertacchi argues that banning iPods will not stop cheating. Cheating, he points out, was around long before iPods. He notes that cheating was just as easy with a $100 calculator and suggests that iPods are being unfairly singled out because they are so trendy. "It shouldn't take a rocket scientist to realize this is the same old problem, just with a new, flashy coat of paint," he writes. He argues that instead of trying to stop cheating by banning electronics, schools should focus on teaching students fundamental skills. Bertacchi is the opinions editor of the *Western Courier*, the student newspaper of Western Illinois University.

First it was baseball caps, then cell phones; now high schools around the country are banning iPods and other digital media players due to their ability to help cheaters. Unfortunately, amid the frantic dash to rip the last remaining joy a high school student has right out of his or her pubescent fingers, education officials have failed to realize they're dealing with a problem that began well before the iPod era: iDiots.

Cheating and/or cutting corners has been part of the American way for the last 20 or 30 years. Nobody likes to admit it, but it's

Michael Bertacchi, "Who's Really Cheating Whom?" *Western Courier*, May 4, 2007. Copyright © 2007 *Western Courier*. Reproduced by permission.

the truth. From professional athletes' use of illegal supplements to achieve more impressive results quickly and easily to America's notorious political landscape, our country is, without a doubt, riddled with cheats, liars and farces. But cheating in high school? Dear Lord, what's this world coming to?

Bans Are Not the Answer

Banning digital media players like iPods will not solve the cheating epidemic. It won't even curb it. Why do I know this? Because there was this thing back when I was in high school called a CD player, and with about the same amount of effort required to make

Two students at Lake Highlands Junior High in Dallas, Texas, use graphing calculators in math class. Some argue that devices like these have been used to cheat at school for decades before iPods became available.

a podcast, you could easily record and burn a CD laced with cheats if you really wanted to. Believe it or not, if someone wanted to cheat prior to the iPod era, he or she could. Cheating was just as rampant 20 years ago as it is today, and the fact that the technology has changed doesn't mean the odds of cheating have spiked dramatically.

Teachers are also finding cheats interwoven in their students' iPod menus. Apparently, they aren't familiar with the capabilities of the $100 graphing calculators most of them require for their courses.

Just the Latest Way Kids Cheat

It shouldn't take a rocket scientist to realize this is the same old problem, just with a new, flashy coat of paint. The only reason this form of cheating is becoming an issue worthy of discussion happens to be because the iPod brand is sexy enough to whip small-minded people into a frenzy. After all, you never saw Texas Instruments in the news in this light, did you? Yet, Texas Instruments is just as guilty (if not more so) as Apple.

The rampancy of cheating and the numerous ways it can be accomplished via electronic devices says a lot about the state of our education system. When did we decide to stop teaching subjects like math and replace them with courses teaching kids how to do math on a calculator that can graph their equations, play vintage Atari games like Pong and save them the hassle of actually using their own minds for a change? Whatever happened to reinforcing real, tangible skills like being able to do complex division?

I'll tell you what happened: The American school system opted to cut some corners. Ironically, in doing so it has cheated America's students out of a solid, cognitive-based education. Funny how things like that work out.

Schools Need to Focus on Basic Skills

Ultimately, something should be said about integrity. It is the single most important thing our current school system neglects. Rather than building future generations around a solid core of

Top 5 "In" Things on Campus

	Spring 2005	Spring 2006
iPods	59%	73%
Drinking Beer	72%	71%
Facebook.com	NA	71%
Drinking other alcohol	65%	67%
Text messaging	59%	66%

Taken from: Student Monitor

fundamental skills, we're propping them up on one crutch after another. If it isn't tangible pieces of equipment like over-priced calculators, it's the way in which students are passed through the system like herds of cattle. Nobody cares whether they're struggling or lacking the required skill sets, just as long as they have a product to sell come harvest.

And until the system stops cheating the students, what incentive do the students have not to cheat the system? It almost seems unfair to expect to measure up to someone's standards when those very same people are neglecting the very integrity they expect their students to showcase.

Do me a favor. Grab a pen or pencil and . . . try to solve this problem without referring to a math book, calculator or a friend: In right triangle ABC, hypotenuse AB=15 and angle A=35°. Find leg BC to the nearest tenth.

And we wonder why kids are cheating these days.

FIVE

Cell Phones Should Be Allowed on School Property

Janne Perona

> Janne Perona argues that a New York City ban on cell phones in school is overkill. She details problems with the ban, such as parental concerns about children not having a cell phone in emergencies. An all-out ban, Perona writes, has too many logistical and constitutional problems to be feasible. A much easier solution, she suggests, is to have students turn off their phones during class. At the writing of this article, Perona was a junior at the University of Arizona, majoring in criminal justice administration.

I, like many of my fellow students, had a cell phone when I was in high school. Now kids as young as 12 or 13 have them. But as technology becomes cheaper and owners get younger, schools institute rules to accommodate. At my high school, the rule was that cell phones could not be out or used while classes were in session. In New York City, it goes a step further and children may not bring cell phones to school period.

The word "overkill" comes to mind, but a few New York City parents thought of another one: unconstitutional.

Eight parents and a citywide parents' association are suing New York City Mayor Michael Bloomberg, Schools Chancellor Joel Klein and the city's Department of Education. They argue that the city ban "is so broad and blunt that it violates their constitutional right as parents to keep their children safe and to raise them in the way they see fit" according to the *New York Times*.

Ban Violates Parents Right

The suit, filed in State Supreme Court in Manhattan, claims that the rule violates the relationship between parents and children without a "compelling education reason" for doing so.

However, the schools chancellor says otherwise. "It is our experience that when cell phones are brought into schools, they are

A sign on the door of Milwaukee's Bradley Tech High School explains the ban on cell phones that was instituted at the school in early 2007.

STOP!

NO CELL PHONES IN SCHOOL

Students are **not allowed to possess** or use two-way electronic communication devices, such as **pagers and cell phones** while on premises controlled by MPS.

USE THEM – AND YOU COULD LOSE THEM.

Cell phones or other communication devices can be confiscated.

If you use a communication device to endanger the physical safety or mental well-being of others, **you could be expelled**.

For additional questions or concerns, please see your school office.

IIIPS
Milwaukee Public Schools

The classroom is the most important place in the district.

used and disrupt the school's learning environment. There is no constitutional right to disrupt a student's education," he wrote in an e-mail to the *New York Times*. In reducing this "distraction," school officials have already confiscated more than 3,000 cell phones in New York City's public schools.

The lawyers representing the parents, Norman Siegel and David Leichtman, emphasized that the parents were not advocating use of cell phones during the school day, only before and after school. Therefore, if it is not being used during school hours, there is no disruption.

If cell phones are "disrupting the educational environment" as Chancellor Klein asserts, then it seems that the proper course of action is to ban their use during school hours, not their presence on school property. Doing so can cause simple safety problems.

An Issue of Safety

Parents say it is a safety concern. Many of the students in New York City's public schools ride buses or subways to get to school, and some have needed to use cell phones to call for help when threatened on the way home or left outside of school alone and locked out. If a student's car battery dies while he is in school, a cell phone makes it easy to call his parents for help (especially in this day and age of speed dial where people don't know phone numbers anymore).

Aside from safety concerns, it is an issue of simple freedoms. Aside from dealing drugs and vandalizing school property, there are few things that students cannot do before or after classes on school property. Talking on their cell phones certainly shouldn't be one of them.

This is one case in a long legacy of cases relating to student rights. How much freedom should students have, and which rights should they be entitled to? Lawyers—and judges—have debated these questions for decades.

History has watched as students have taken on school districts for basic constitutional rights, including the right to have certain types of clubs on campus, the right to peacefully protest

Kids and Cell Phones at St. Petersburg High School

- 95% have cell phones
- 97% of those who have cell phones bring them to school.
- 88% know the district's policy on cell phone use.
- 90% of students who know the policy disobey it.
- 95% of the students who disobey the rule text message during class.
- 24% say they have used their cell phones to cheat.
- 28% say they have had their cell phones confiscated.

Taken from: *St. Petersburg Times*

government and the right to not salute the flag during morning recitations of the Pledge of Allegiance.

Now, parents are fighting for their students' rights to possess a piece of electronic equipment that is neither dangerous nor lethal. It's certainly not as lofty as religious freedom, but sadly, it has become necessary.

Schools are faced with increasing pressure to raise standards and test scores yet bombarded with changing social norms—such as children owning cell phones at a younger age.

However, in an attempt to keep order in the schoolroom, administrators have stepped outside the realm of feasibility. There are just too many problems, both logistically and constitutionally, with an all-out ban on cell phones on public school grounds.

It is admirable that schools are trying to cut down on distractions in the classroom, but in my experience, the two girls sitting behind me talking to each other (in person, not on their cell phones) are a bigger distraction than anything. Let kids use their cell phones in the hallways, but have them check them (or turn them off) at the classroom door.

SIX

The Cell Phone Ban Needs Rethinking

Ellen Song

In the following viewpoint Ellen Song discusses the unpopular New York City ban on cell phones in schools. She lists the most common arguments that proponents of the plan make, and explains why those arguments are flawed. For example, she tackles the argument that students did not always carry cell phones and therefore do not need them. Song equates cell phones to other technological devices such as vacuum cleaners and washing machines—although they are arguably not necessities, they are great conveniences, and we have come to rely on them. As she notes, "cell phones serve as a link between parents and students in an often alienating city, one in which considerable thousands of students must commute to school every single day, with commutes sometimes lasting close to two hours. . . . Why deprive us of the ability to call our parents—and other loved ones—in times of possible crisis or emergency?" As this book went to press, the ban was still in effect but facing legal challenges. Ellen Song is the secretary and senior editor for the *BTHSnews* (Brooklyn Tech High School newspaper).

In today's technologically-advanced, fast-paced world, having certain types of technology at hand is no longer an advantage; rather, it is a disadvantage not to have them. The computer is a prime example of this, as students are generally expected to have at-home access to a computer with internet connection.

With this belief, teachers assign research projects, essays, and the like, expecting the assignments to be typed up on white, unruled paper, not handwritten on looseleaf. However, the computer is not a "vital" need, especially not according to [psychologist Abraham] Maslow's Hierarchy of Needs. The computer is not food, it does not nourish. It is not clothing, it does not protect our skin from the roughness of the world. It does not provide us with a sense of spirituality. Frankly put, it is not a need, the word *need* indicating necessity for survival.

Neither is the cellphone. At least, not according to the Department of Education and Mayor Bloomberg. The DoE and Mayor Bloomberg seem to be under the impression that the cellphone is not truly important in the life of a New York City student, and that in due time, city kids will just learn to deal with the ban that remains in place since 1988, for fear of having their precious cellphones confiscated. Many school administrators and staff are countering angry parents who claim the cellphone is a "vital lifeline" between parents and children, with statements such as *"Students have gone to school for ages without the use of electronics,"* or *"Cellphones promote cheating and stealing"* and *"Cellphones are a distraction in the classroom."* However, there are altogether too many things that proponents of the citywide cellphone ban are overlooking.

"Students Did Not Always Carry Cellphones to School"

"Students did not always carry cellphones to school, and therefore, they do not need it now either." This serves as a true statement, since cellphones became ubiquitous only within the last decade. Yet as the advances of technology increase, so do the "needs" of the public. For example, we did not always rely on washing machines to

get the laundry done, or the air conditioner to keep us cool in the summers. We should stop using our vacuum cleaners in favor of the old broom and dustpan. Our forefathers functioned just fine without them, so can't we do the same? No, obviously we cannot. Although these machines are not direly necessary for survival, they do serve as great time-saving conveniences, and in that sense, we are wholly dependent on them.

Such is the way we are dependent on our cellphones. Cellphones serve as a link between parents and students in an

Steven Cao is a student in the New York City school system, where cell phones were not allowed in 2006, but his mother insists that he carry a phone to school anyway so she can stay in touch with him.

often alienating city, one in which considerable thousands of students must commute to school every single day, with commutes sometimes lasting close to two hours. After the London train bombings, no one knows what to expect of train rides. September 11th showed us how important cellphones are, as people rushed to call their loved ones, whether it was to say a final goodbye, or to check up on family and friends. Why deprive us of the ability to call our parents—and other loved ones—in times of possible crisis or emergency, regardless of it being a citywide terrorist attack or an unfortunate medical emergency?

Furthermore, cellphones can be vital to students in other ways, *after* school. In an age where high grades and SAT scores will not guarantee acceptance into top-notch colleges, many students take on extra responsibilities: internships, jobs, community service, etc. Why should we be denied the opportunity to call a potential employer to schedule an appointment (before their offices close) or tell a boss that, due to unseen circumstances, we'll be late to work? *"Use a payphone,"* some staff members say. *"Ask a teacher to let you use a department office phone."* There are no payphones at our own school, and to find a pay-

Parents' Opinion on Cell Phones at School

- 99% want to be able to contact their children and have their children contact them via cell phone in an emergency.

- 99% want their children to be able to contact them by cell phone if a dangerous situation arises on the way to or from school.

- 84% want to be able to contact their children and have their children contact them via cell phone during school hours if there is a schedule change.

- 71% of parents say their children need a cell phone at school because school administrators won't allow them to use the office phone except in case of illness or emergency.

Taken from: ACE*COMM Corp.

phone that actually works instead of eating up 50 cents is quite difficult today. There have been many occasions after school when I've had to pass by a department office, and discovered that it was empty. Who will help me make a phone call in such situations?

Translator Issues

"If there is an emergency, parents can call the school to reach their children." That would be nice, but sadly, many parents do not speak English, or cannot sacrifice too much time to wait for the phone call to go through, have someone pick up on the school's end, transfer the call to the student's guidance counselor, who will then attempt to notify the child's teacher, and so on, so forth. *"There will be someone at school who can translate for non-English speaking parents."* If this is so, how easy will it be to find an appropriate translator? I already know that there is no one in the administration who can translate for my own parents, as my parents' native language is not one that is popular even among the diverse Tech student body. Moreover, how many different languages can our translators speak? Certainly not enough to accommodate the needs of every single student in our huge school.

"Cellphones promote cheating and stealing." Let's face it. Cheating is never going to go away; students have cheated for ages, and will continue to do so. And surely, we can hope, that any teacher administering an exam will be attentive enough to notice a student trying to cheat by text messaging his friends for answers. Simply put, confiscating cellphones will not eradicate or lessen cheating, as students who rely on cheating will continue to rely on cheating, cellphone or no cellphone. As for the notion that asserts cellphones promote stealing, cellphones are not the only expensive items students will bring to school. Under this argument, students should not be wearing expensive jewelry or clothing, for such items may be stolen just as well. Even graphing calculators, which are indeed allowed in schools, cost over $100, the usual price tag for a quality cellphone.

Teachers Can Have Phones—Why Not Students?

Finally, *"Cellphones are a distraction in the classroom."* My teachers' phones, which are not turned off, have rung in class several times. Even after the phones ring, some teachers do not turn them off or put them on silent mode, as the phones tend to ring again shortly. In some instances, the teacher even answers the call. While such actions are justified by saying that the call may be very important, the same argument can be used to support students' needs for cellphones in schools. As for distractions caused by the students themselves, I have often observed that kids who use their phones during class to play games or send text messages are better off keeping themselves preoccupied by doing just that, instead of talking to other students around them and disrupting the whole lesson. Removing cellphones will not cause students to pay more attention in class.

It is ironic that New York City, arguably the busiest, most bustling city in the nation, is banning the use of cellphones in schools, even though the device is clearly indispensable to students, parents, and other individuals. We have become so dependent on the cellphone that taking it away from us will undoubtedly have a negative impact on our lives. Taking away our phones, ultimately, is the ban that will take us one step backward from the technological progress we have made up until today.

SEVEN

Camera Phones Create a Spylike Culture

Rafi Martina

> In this selection Rafi Martina warns that cameras are watching all of us. The source of these cameras? "I speak of nothing other than the digital cameras and camera-phones nestled in the pockets of nearly all of my peers," he writes. Martina argues this constant surveillance changes the way we behave. "Like an eight-year-old hamming it up for the family video camera, once-earnest acts become mere contrivances," he notes. He argues that the cameras also rob us of our power in creating memories and allow only one version—the camera's. Martina is a writer for the *Michigan Daily*.

Beware, comrades: We're living in a panoptic [allowing people to be observed without them knowing they are being observed] society. With cameras and video cameras in every classroom, any action potentially draws their gaze. Anything spontaneous, anything out of the ordinary and click—at least one of them is going to catch it.

Perhaps the greatest irony in this panoptic society is the fact that we've done it to ourselves. While [eighteenth-century English philosopher] Jeremy Bentham envisioned a society in which governments spied on their subjects (particularly in relation to

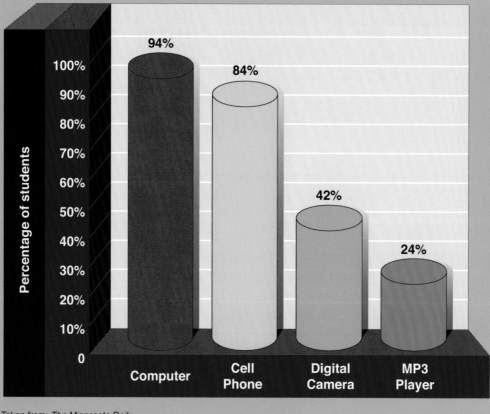

Students Owning Electronic Devices at the University of Minnesota

Percentage of students

- 94% Computer
- 84% Cell Phone
- 42% Digital Camera
- 24% MP3 Player

Taken from: *The Minnesota Daily*

punitive measures), the gaze of the panopticon is rather self-inflicted in our case. Those cameras in our classrooms? I speak of nothing other than the digital cameras and camera-phones nestled in the pockets of nearly all of my peers.

By nonchalantly pressing a button, any of us can discreetly (might I even say surreptitiously) record our surroundings, even going so far as to publish—or, in common parlance, "post"—a record of that surveillance on the Internet. With both the proliferation of post-it-yourself video sites and the low cost of caching information found on the Web, it hardly needs reminding that the momentarily hilarious video of you defecating on someone's porch becomes an indelible record of your, shall we say, lapsed judgment. No, Big Brother isn't watching you, but that friend of your older brother who you've always hated might be—and he might just send your brother (or mother) the video of, say, you puking after a late Saturday night. Indeed, many of you might not know you've been reconnoitered until you unexpectedly come upon it on YouTube.com.

Constant Surveillance Changes Behavior

Undoubtedly all this talk of a panoptic society sounds rather alarmist, perhaps even paranoid. But I ask you to consider for a moment the effect such ostensibly benign surveillance has on something as basic as life itself. Perhaps I romanticize that concept too much, but when actions must anticipate the potential of being captured, the very spontaneity and impulsiveness that inspire hilarity or unforgettable moments are lost. It might not even be overly philosophical to suppose that the presumption of being watched (which inevitably affects one's decision-making and actions) inhibits our free will. Like an eight-year-old hamming it up for the family video camera, once-earnest acts become mere contrivances.

To be sure, much of the entertainment in witnessing unscripted acts in life comes from their ephemeral nature: They are unpredictable and nearly impossible to reenact. And much of their charm comes in the sometimes fumbling act of retelling such memorable events.

Without videography, every witness to an interesting event becomes an empowered part of that event, rather than a casual and ancillary blur in an image of that event. It is the power of retelling an interesting event—without the formalism inherent in a filmed version—that makes life worth recounting. But by yielding to technology to do the work for us, we abdicate our roles as storytellers: Every one of us is a potential witness to a great event. So too are we all potential raconteurs of such events. And the beauty is in the plurality of perspectives that such recounting leaves us—in contrast to videography that yields only a singular retelling. When we can play someone else's video of an interesting occurrence with greater ease than giving our own recounting of that event, we become merely an audience in our own lives, giving others the responsibility (and power) of crafting our own memories.

Camera Phones Do Some Good, but . . .

Sure, camera phones have served the purposes of amateur journalism. The would-be sleuths who captured the use of a Taser on

Some argue that with cameras everywhere, privacy is hard to come by and that people are changing their behavior because of the assumption they will be captured in a photo.

a harmless student at UCLA is a case in point. The videographer capturing Michael Richards's racist tirade is another case in which camera phones proved effective in giving witness to an egregious act. George Allen's "macaca" remark serves as another example.

But relative to the enormous cache of amateur-filmed events—banal videos of everyday life included—such instances appear more as the exception than the rule. Just like the panopticon crafted to monitor grievous acts such as those above, the unintended consequence of viewing everything has a rather pernicious effect on our lives. While no overly aggressive UCLA policeman is likely to stun a hapless student with a Taser again, while no moronic politician will likely utter an ethnic slur in public, the prominence of camera phones hasn't made those policemen docile or cured Allen of his racism.

No, the panopticon has merely made fumbling public figures more deliberative in public. Stump speeches won't deviate from scripts. Policemen will conduct their business more mechanically. The presence of camera phones has merely demanded all of us not to let our guards down. But the novelty of capturing once-candid happenings is lost when all public displays become charades of inauthentic decorum.

If I may be so bold as to offer one suggestion: Allow life to play out both unscripted and unfilmed.

EIGHT

Students with Cameras Keep Teachers on Good Behavior

Todd Seal

> The following essay deals with the phenomenon of students using electronic devices to make surreptitious videos of their teachers, then posting the videos on YouTube. Some schools have responded by banning all electronic devices with camera and video capabilities. Todd Seal, a teacher, argues that cameras in school are not the problem—angry teachers who berate their classes are. He thinks that camera phones could help keep teacher behavior in check and offers the suggestion that schools could even help students post their teacher videos.

Students! Do you have a video camera on your cell phone? Bring it! All I ask is that before you post anything about me to YouTube, let me know and send me a copy of it. Send it to me anonymously if you're scared of repercussions (but I never let personal feelings affect grades). I need to know what I'm doing so I can make changes or prepare explanations.

Teachers! Do you blow up at your students? Then you deserve to be on YouTube! Get a hold of yourself and start acting like professionals.

So here's the deal: my union wrote a warning in a recent newsletter about students with cameras, advising teachers to be

Todd Seal, "Camera Phone? Bring It!" *Thoughts on Teaching*, April 15, 2007. Reproduced by permission.

aware and even to go so far as to institute policy prohibiting use of them. Really, it should have been a warning to angry teachers. It should have been a notice to teachers that they need to behave, that they need to focus on their job and handle stress in a more positive fashion.

Camera Phones Not the Problem . . . Angry Teachers Are

Camera phones aren't the problem. Angry teachers who berate their classes are. I watched a few of those videos on YouTube (just

A Nokia N73 cell phone with a built-in digital camera is displayed at a store in New York City.

[look] and you'll find 'em) and they disturbed me. That kind of behavior *should* be documented.

I don't mind knowing that my behavior could be caught on a student's camera and posted for the rest of the world to see. That pressure just might keep certain teachers in check. For the rest of us, we don't have anything to worry about. A video of a teacher running a class in a typical manner doesn't make for good YouTube fodder.

What if school districts and teacher unions embraced this phenomenon? What if there were sites set up for students to submit their footage for review by the district or union? Sure, this wouldn't stop students from posting these videos to YouTube. In fact, the school site could be set up just to submit links to videos already on YouTube.

What I'd like to see is students put in the position to use their technology to inform those who need to know. That video students took of the latest fight could be useful in trying to prosecute and identify those involved. It also would allow administration to know what's out there and prepare appropriate ways to respond.

The information, much like the spice, must flow. Schools need to be prepared to receive information just as readily as they dish it out.

NINE

YouTube Belongs in the Classroom

Stan Beer

> Stan Beer, a cofounder and editor in chief of iTWire,
> wrote the following essay in response to a move by the
> State Government of Victoria, Australia, banning
> YouTube from schools. The ban was intended to prevent
> cyber-bullying. Beer, who approaches the issue from the
> perspective of a technology maven, calls the ban "stupid."
> He argues that YouTube is an "extraordinary tool," one
> that can put the powers of video production and mass
> distribution in the hands of anyone. Like any tool, he
> argues, it can be used for good or evil and that banning
> it is "ill-informed."

The State Government of Victoria Australia has taken what
I would consider to be a most stupid and ill-informed step by
banning video sharing site YouTube from schools. The reason
given—to prevent cyber-bullying—is equally stupid and ill-
informed.

[In 2006], some schoolboy thugs made headlines in Australia
and shocked the nation when they tortured a teenage girl in front
of a camera. They made DVDs of the terrible incident, which they
later distributed, and then posted the video to YouTube.

Stan Beer, "Why Not Ban the Internet at Schools?" *www.iTWire.com.au*, March 1, 2007.
Reproduced by permission.

In the US, social networking site MySpace has legislators up in arms because young teenagers pretending to be older than they are have been lured by predators pretending to be something other than they are into dangerous situations with tragic results.

There's no question about it, the Internet can be a dangerous place for the unwary. Chatrooms, instant messaging networks, emails and even merely web browsing can all be dangerous activities if misused. Should we ban them from schools and public libraries?

Absolutely not! Should we teach children how to use the internet safely and in the process reap its benefits and rewards? Absolutely!

YouTube Is an "Extraordinary Tool"

YouTube has become something of a phenomenon on the net. . . . This extraordinary tool has actually put the power of video production and global distribution into the hands of ordinary people. What was once the exclusive franchise of the elite is now within reach of the common folk.

However, like everything else on the net, YouTube can be used for good and for evil. A teacher can make a video of an experiment demonstrating an important scientific principle or deliver a lecture on an economics theory and teachers on the other side of the world can replay the video in class or point students to it for after class viewing.

A student can make a video production for a school project and later post it to YouTube for his or her friends and family all over the world to see. A school could post a video of their annual school play to YouTube. In fact, YouTube can be used as an inexpensive platform to teach students the art of film making.

Alternatively, a bunch of ratbag boys can video their abuse of a helpless young girl and post it to YouTube. Did they post it to YouTube at school or at home? Does it matter? Did thuggish classmates view it at school or at home? Does it matter? It was a criminal act well before it made it to YouTube.

Cyber-bullying is a problem, no doubt about it. But why single out YouTube? Email, SMS [short message service; sending short messages to and from mobile phones] instant messaging, social

In one example of a positive use for YouTube, police officer Brian Johnson uploaded a surveillance video of a crime to the site hoping that someone who viewed it online could help identify the perpetrators.

networking sites where jilted boyfriends and girlfriends slander their ex are all far more culpable mediums for cyber-bullying. Mobile phones have hit the news recently in the US as being an especially abused medium by teenagers bullying and intimidating other teenagers.

However, YouTube is not like a mobile phone. You can't send an intimidating instant message or email to a classmate on YouTube. In fact, it was YouTube that exposed the schoolboy thugs to [the] world and brought them down. In an act of hubris and immature bravado, they uploaded their crime

Most Popular Video Search Sites

Rank	Name	Domain	Market Share	Avg Visit (mins)
1	YouTube	www.youtube.com	42.94%	13.20
2	MySpace Videos	vids.myspace.com	24.22%	4.41
3	Yahoo! Video Search	video.yahoo.com	9.58%	15.02
4	MSN Video Search	video.msn.com	9.21%	2.58
5	Google Video	video.google.com	6.48%	7.44
6	AOL Video	us.video.aol.com	4.28%	6.41
7	iFilm	www.ifilm.com	2.28%	6.14
8	Grouper	www.grouper.com	0.69%	5.02
9	Dailymotion.com	www.dailymotion.com	0.22%	11.31
10	vSocial.com	www.vsocial.com	0.09%	7.14

Taken from: Hitwise

for the world to see and thankfully were collared for their efforts.

So please explain to the world, Education Services Minister for the State of Victoria Jacinta Allan, exactly how will banning the use of one of the most innovative applications for the global distribution of video information at schools decrease cyber-bullying? Why not just simply ban the use of the Internet?

TEN

Classroom Activities Should Not Be on YouTube

Scott Jaschik

In the following piece Scott Jaschik writes about the issue of students posting videos of their teachers on YouTube from the perspective of the teachers. Some teachers, he notes, do not even know they have become "stars" of such videos. He quotes the blog Metaspencer, which warns teachers, "Were you videotaped in front of your class yesterday? Today? Will what you do with your students be edited and presented in a way that you feel misrepresents how you teach?" Jaschik touches on legal issues such as whether such videos are an expression of free speech and notes that the practice is making teachers feel more unsteady about their job security. Jaschik is the editor of *Inside Higher Ed.*

If you don't like what RateMyProfessors.com has done for the image of professors, get ready for the YouTube effect. YouTube is the immensely popular Web site where people post videos of themselves and their friends hanging out, doing mock television shows, watching television, or just about anything you can imagine in front of a video camera of some sort.

Because YouTube is very popular with college students, it should probably come as no surprise that they are posting videos of course scenes on the Web site—and judging from interviews with the "stars" of these postings, the professors aren't being asked or giving permission for the filming. Nonetheless, some of the videos feature professors' names, disciplines and institutions.

Judith Thorpe, who just retired from teaching at the University of Wisconsin at Oshkosh, had no idea that someone had filmed her class and posted it, with her name. Matt Kearly had no idea that what claims to be a biology lecture he gave this month at Auburn University had been posted. In other cases, professors aren't named, but they are clearly visible and held up to ridicule—as in the video of a professor who is not a native speaker of English mispronouncing a word repeatedly, and made fun of by the student who posted the video. The word is "glucocorticoids"—not a word many non-experts would necessarily use with ease.

To be sure, many of the videos of campus scenes are from public events—protests, strikes, inaugurations. And many more are

On March 13, 2007, the entertainment company Viacom sued YouTube, claiming that by allowing users to post copyrighted Viacom material, it had violated Viacom's intellectual property rights.

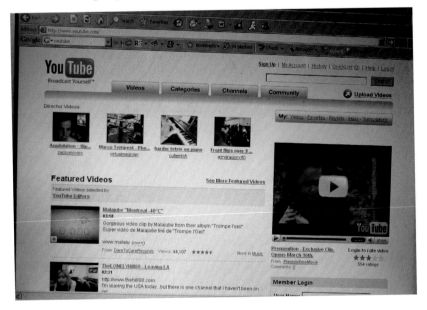

just silly and don't invade anyone's privacy. But many others involve filming courses, or staging events in courses. The boredom of lectures is a frequent theme, with audio of a professor talking while students look bored—or in the case of one student at Southern Methodist University, fight a losing battle to stay awake.

Classroom Hijinks a Common Theme

Hijinks are also common, in many cases interrupting classes. There's the student who talks about honoring his great grandfather's birthday by mooning a large lecture class. (Warning/spoiler: He goes through with it, so the link may be more detail than you want.) Indiana University students revel at Halloween by interrupting classes as the Village People or portraying scenes from Ghostbusters.

To colleges and faculty members, the filming raises a variety of issues—with regard to their intellectual property and their dignity. Many colleges have been warning students about the images they post of themselves and their friends on YouTube, telling them that scenes of drinking and partying that seem amusing in a dormitory room may not go over well with potential employers. But colleges' focus has been on telling students about the harm they may be doing to themselves, not their professors.

YouTube, whose officials did not respond to phone calls or e-mail messages about this story, posts a variety of warnings on its site about how people should post only those videos for which they have ownership rights, and that it will not post "hateful" videos, among other categories barred by its terms of service. There is also a form someone can fill out to object to a video posting of them, if they own the copyright.

Of course, people who were never asked if they could be filmed in class wouldn't know that they had reason to check what is on the site.

Ann Springer, staff counsel for the American Association of University Professors, said that no professor should be filmed in class without granting permission. "The professor's presentation in class is the professor's intellectual property, and to submit it to

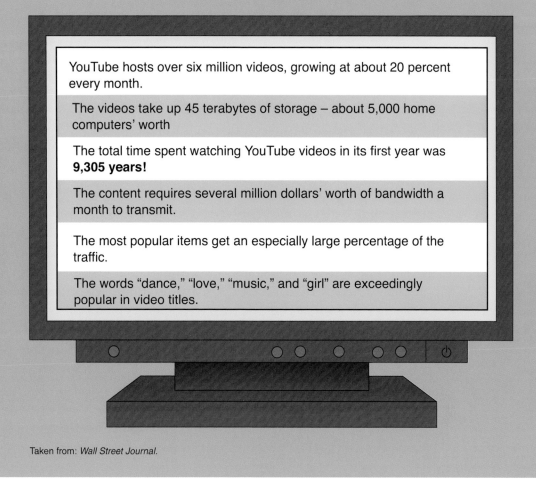

YouTube by the Numbers

YouTube hosts over six million videos, growing at about 20 percent every month.

The videos take up 45 terabytes of storage – about 5,000 home computers' worth

The total time spent watching YouTube videos in its first year was **9,305 years!**

The content requires several million dollars' worth of bandwidth a month to transmit.

The most popular items get an especially large percentage of the traffic.

The words "dance," "love," "music," and "girl" are exceedingly popular in video titles.

Taken from: *Wall Street Journal.*

a Web site is a violation of those rights—and a concern to the university and the professor," she said. If a competing college started posting video of a professor's courses, that would be a violation of rights, and the same legal principles apply, regardless of whether there is profit involved, Springer said.

Filming Teachers Is Not a Free Speech Issue

She stressed that this wasn't a free speech issue. "Students will always mock professors and there's nothing you can do about that," she said. But filming them without permission is the issue, whatever the use of the video.

In cases where taping of professors has become public—generally when the taping was politically motivated, not just for the purpose of mocking—universities have responded, she noted. In January [2006], for example, a conservative group at the University of California at Los Angeles offered to pay students to tape professors, with the idea of exposing alleged ideological bias. The group backed down when the university and faculty groups raised intellectual property issues.

A spokesman for Indiana University said that the institution has received no complaints from professors about having their lectures filmed, but that university officials would consider it a violation of rules barring "disorderly conduct" or behavior that interferes with teaching. University policy gives professors the right to permit or reject any photography or taping in their classes.

Aside from the legal issues, there are also questions to some academics about how this YouTube trend affects professors generally, and whether anything can be done about it. Neil Gross, a sociologist at Harvard University, has surveyed public attitudes about faculty members, and found "soft support" for their work, and skepticism of some of their views. He said that in the mocking of professors on YouTube, he saw some strains of political disagreement with professors, along with "classic anti-intellectual themes, as well as the typical youthful distaste for authority."

The Implications for Teachers

Several academic blogs, such as Yellow Dog and Digital Digs, have been discussing the implications as they relate to both professors and high school teachers (videos abound on YouTube of teachers losing their temper in class, for instance). Among the issues being raised are whether this form of expression—however upsetting to faculty members—is an example of students acting on their feelings and expressing themselves, something composition instructors in particular tend to encourage.

The blog Metaspencer predicted that YouTube would have an impact that builds on the way RateMyProfessors.com has intimidated many faculty members—who hate the site and check to see how they are doing on it.

"When that site first went online, many seemed outraged that college level instructors would be publicly assessed in this way, outside of our already established course-evaluation-systems, and in many cases, professors have been graphically slandered and bodily objectified on that site. RateMyProfessors.com made our lives as college level instructors suddenly unstable and encouraged some of us to be just a bit more careful, if that's the right word, when it comes to what we do in the classroom," the blog said. "Videos of teachers on YouTube, however, magnify whatever paranoia RateMyProfessors.com may have generated. Were you videotaped in front of your class yesterday? Today? Will what you do with your students be edited and presented in a way that you feel misrepresents how you teach?"

ELEVEN

Teachers Should Not Ban Students from Being Online in Class

Ken Fisher

In the following selection Ken Fisher writes about the efforts made by schools and teachers to control students who use laptops to go online for nonschool purposes during class time. He points to one school that has given its professors the capabilities to block Internet access "with the flip of a switch." Such efforts are futile, he argues, since new technologies can and will allow students to override such blocks. People who urge teachers to make their lectures more interesting are also missing the point. No matter how interesting a professor's lecture is, he writes, a single person can never compete with the wealth of knowledge the Internet offers. The key for teachers, he suggests, is to accept that there will be students in the class watching *Snakes on a Plane!* and, if possible, try to work it into the lecture. In the end, a student's grades will determine how much in-class time they want to spend online. Fisher is a self-described "technologist" and an educator.

In the early nineties, laptop in tow, I was almost always co-computing with at least two or three other people in every class. The real ubiquity of laptops in the classroom didn't come until much later for me, when I was no longer taking classes but teaching them. In my own experience, it wasn't the convenience of a laptop or its impressive capabilities that was driving student usage.

It was WiFi.

Today that is still the case. As a lecturer peers out at her students, of those with a laptop one can be sure that at least a third of them are gripped by and totally fixated on the new information they're taking in . . . at *The Drudge Report* [news Web site consisting of links to currents events media].

Professors, academic deans, and even university IT staff are now finding themselves in a 'Net neutrality battle of their own, but this one might be better characterized as *Pedagogy vs. The Intraweb*. The same schools that rushed to bring "WiFi to Campus" are now turning it off, creating new policies, or rethinking their implementations. In rare instances, professors are banning laptops from the classroom altogether. Others have taken the approach of asking students to close laptops for periods of time, while others are looking for ways to remind students that participation in class is required—big screen in front of your face or not.

Giving Professors Control

Another approach, as reported by the *Chronicle of Higher Education*, is being tested at Bentley College. There professors have been given the keys to the Internet kingdom, and with a flip of a switch can knock out WiFi in their classrooms.

> Called the "classroom network control system," it allows professors in many classrooms to choose one of five settings: turn off Internet access but allow e-mail access, turn off e-mail access but allow Internet access, disable Internet and e-mail access but allow computers to reach campus Web pages, shut off all access, or allow all access. A computer at the front of the classroom lets the professor change the settings at any time.

The system at Bentley is actually several years old, although it was only recently modified to allow professors to shut off WiFi in addition to wired Ethernet. Reportedly, they are able to turn off WiFi rather effectively, without significant problems stemming from active WiFi signals at nearby locations. Phillip G. Knutel, director of academic technology at Bentley, says that professors have really taken to the system. They shouldn't get too comfortable, however.

An Important Note

The *Chronicle* article misses one very important detail in this: the foolhardiness of controlling access to the Internet. The days

Students work on wireless laptops during a class at Harrisburg University in Pennsylvania. Some argue that it is impossible to keep students offline in the classroom.

of controlling Internet access via your college's or university's WiFi infrastructure are coming to an end shortly after they started. Telecommunications companies such as Verizon already offer high-speed wireless EVDO [technology that allows transmission of data through radio signals] to laptop users in major metropolitan cities, and short of violating federal law, schools cannot block those signals. In just a few short years, most laptops will likely come with support for commercial networks much in the way that they now come with support for WiFi. Laptops already ship with EVDO support, and WiMax support is around the corner. As prices drop (and they will), students will be as connected to the Internet as they are to their friends via mobile phones.

Stopping the Internet Is a "Waste of Time"

As both a technologist and an educator myself, I see both sides of the debate, but stopping the Internet from getting into the classroom is a waste of time. Students are not going to tolerate laptop bans in the classroom, especially in undergraduate education (graduate education is slightly different because of the changes in interpersonal dynamics that come along with it). Professors are going to have to deal with the frustration of seeing their students giggling about "Snakes on a Plane!" during their lectures on Stoic passions. (Unless I happen to be teaching, at which point I'll work the "Snakes on a Plane!" into the talk about the Stoic passions, just to keep everyone alert.)

While calls to make education "more interesting" are commonly offered as the solution to what ails the classroom full of web surfers, such demagoguery falls flat on its face the minute one remembers that students' interests are as broad if not broader than the collegiate curriculum itself. Without a doubt, some rusty old professors haven't said anything new or interesting to their students since 1965, but that's cold comfort to professors who are aware that teaching almost *any topic* next to the *practically unlimited offerings available online* is a challenge in terms of fighting the wandering mind.

Changes in the Classroom After a Laptop Program in Maine

Changes after laptop program	More often	About as often	Less often
Students explore a topic on their own	61%	29%	10%
Students write more than one page	59%	32%	9%
Students present their work in class	58%	36%	6%
Students engage in multiple activities during class	44%	44%	12%
Students select their own research areas	41%	39%	20%
Students teach other students	40%	36%	24%
Students work in groups	38%	53%	9%
Students teach the teacher	33%	31%	36%
Teachers make connections across classes	23%	61%	16%
Student interests influence lessons	23%	56%	21%
Direct instruction by teachers	19%	65%	17%
Quizzes and tests	17%	67%	16%
Students answer textbook questions	14%	60%	26%
A textbook is the primary guide	6%	53%	41%

Taken from: Mitchell Institute/ Bill & Melinda Gates Foundation.

What can you do in the face of blocking efforts that ultimately will fail? Really, professors shouldn't be doing anything new. A well-structured class should have a lecture component that delivers material and analysis necessary for the student's performance in the course. The bigger question is, if Joe Baccalaureate got through Econ 101 with an "A" while spending his time manicuring his rotisserie-style fantasy baseball team in lecture, what was the lecture for to begin with?

TWELVE

Laptops for All Students Should Be Standard

Mark A. Edwards

In the following viewpoint Mark A. Edwards, the superintendent of a school district that provided laptops to each student, writes about the benefits of the program. He points to engaged students, rising test scores, and access to the world's knowledge via the Internet. "Deploying 25,000 wireless-capable laptops," he writes, "has engaged our students, enlivened the learning environment, and moved us toward the kind of equity of opportunity that ought to be at the heart of our democracy." He offers suggestions on how to successfully implement similar programs, including tips like, "Listen to and train teachers," and "Think big." Edwards, the superintendent of Henrico County Public Schools in Virginia, was a recipient of an eSchool News Tech-Savvy Superintendent Award and a McGraw Prize in Education.

As schools across America work to lift student achievement, the effect of technology in the classroom remains the subject of heated debate. One experience in Henrico County, Va., sheds light on the power of technology to improve student learning.

If you want to see how technology expands the bounds of learning, you can look not only in our classrooms, but also at our track meets, school bus stops, and other places around Henrico County where students have their laptops open and their minds engaged. When we witness the effect of providing every student in grades 6–12 and every teacher with a laptop, what is striking is not just where our youngsters are studying but how much they are learning, as their steadily rising scores on rigorous assessments show.

We are now in the third year of this Teaching and Learning Initiative. Whether you take our measure anecdotally or analytically, it is evident that the power of educational technology is fulfilling its promise in Henrico County and creating a community of learners.

Laptops Engage Students

Deploying 25,000 wireless-capable laptops has engaged our students, enlivened the learning environment, and moved us toward the kind of equity of opportunity that ought to be at the heart of our democracy.

We believed—and now we can demonstrate—that providing universal access to laptops at the middle and high school level connects students to their school work in powerful new ways. This 24-7 access facilitates the kind of hands-on, creative environment where students learn best.

We wanted to move away from a sedentary learning style to a more constructivist approach. We wanted, that is, fewer lectures and more engaged, active learning using dynamic, current content. We knew from experience that students learn best as active learners.

Today, in many of our classrooms, there is a new sense of discovery and the feel of a research laboratory. Every student has access to a universe of online libraries. A class exploring Italian Renaissance artists, for example, reaches a depth and breadth of study well beyond what they would have been exposed to previously.

As a former biology teacher, I was delighted to observe a lab simulation of a frog dissection that represented a great leap forward over what had been possible before in lab instruction. What had been a once-a-year, two-hour experience was now a learning project that could be taken apart and reassembled in the classroom or at home. It is no surprise that student performance in 10th grade biology has increased dramatically.

Students Can Take Advantage of Online Content

Our students benefit from the impressive evolution of online content—from lab simulations to dynamic notation in mathematics to virtual museum tours. At the same time, we continue to see a role for more traditional materials. Technology cannot replace the pleasure of turning the pages of Julius Caesar—or Harry Potter.

Students use their iBook laptops in class at Tucker High School in Henrico County, Virginia. Henrico County was the first school district in the nation to provide laptops to all of its students.

Technology can build badly-needed connections between the school and the home. At the middle school level, we have required training for parents before students can get their laptops. Given that parental involvement in education traditionally falls off sharply in the middle and high school years, this training can serve a dual purpose: ensuring proper use of the computer and strengthening the link between family and school.

This initiative is also a force for equal opportunity. Providing every student with a laptop bridges the digital divide. About one-third of our county's population—and a far higher share of our minority families—lacked home access to the internet before we began this project. Today, the Technology and Learning Initiative provides the opportunity for universal internet access at home for nearly all Henrico County parents.

In the areas where we have used the laptops most extensively, such as English, our students have registered large gains on the Virginia Standards of Learning (SOL) program. On a countywide basis, we have a pass rate of more than 96 percent in English, which at the high school level is a composite of writing, English, and reading. In world history, where our pass rate also exceeds 97 percent, our department chairs and curriculum specialists have developed localized online content.

Every regular school in Henrico County is now fully accredited under the SOL program. Our high school students have improved . . . in all 11 of the end-of-year SOL tests. The composite pass rate of these tests now exceeds 90 percent.

Creating Successful Programs

While every school district is distinct, our experience suggests that these guiding principles are instrumental to the success of such a program:

Think big.

Even though we had previously expended millions of dollars on technology, we were not having the impact we sought. We concluded that having that impact required a one-to-one ratio

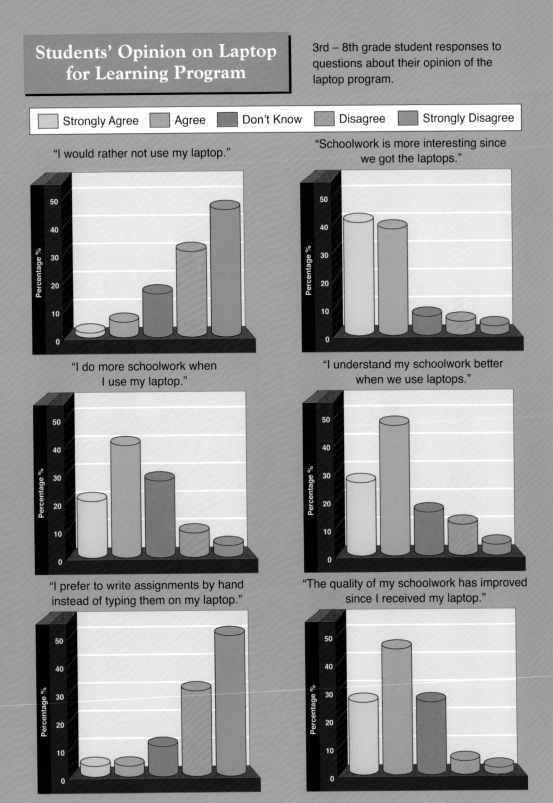

Students' Opinion on Laptop for Learning Program

3rd – 8th grade student responses to questions about their opinion of the laptop program.

Strongly Agree   Agree   Don't Know   Disagree   Strongly Disagree

"I would rather not use my laptop."

"Schoolwork is more interesting since we got the laptops."

"I do more schoolwork when I use my laptop."

"I understand my schoolwork better when we use laptops."

"I prefer to write assignments by hand instead of typing them on my laptop."

"The quality of my schoolwork has improved since I received my laptop."

Taken from: University of California at Irvine.

between students and computers. We also believed that if we aggressively sought a business partner, we could achieve that ratio.

Find a business partner.
We told potential corporate partners that we could become a living laboratory for the effects of universal student access to high-quality technology. We met with Apple CEO Steve Jobs, who told us he had been waiting for just such an opportunity on a district-wide basis.

Sweat the details.
The most important detail is the state of the infrastructure. In our first year of deployment, our key issue was network capability.

Listen to and train teachers.
At the heart of our laptop program is a firm commitment to teacher training. Embracing the concept of a learning community means giving teachers the skills and tools they need to be effective. Middle school teachers received their laptops a full year before deployment. By the time students got their computers, the teachers had a very high degree of confidence that they could make this program work.

Enlist the broadest possible support.
Before implementing the program, we met with a leadership team—consisting of principals, teachers, and students—from each of our seven high schools. We told them we were thinking of piloting the laptop program in a few schools. Their response, in every case, was that their school could take on this challenge. Instead of a pilot project, we had a pioneering spirit to carry out this program across the board.

We also met with PTA presidents from every school and with business and community leaders. All groups encouraged us to move forward. When we hit a few bumps on the trail early on, our business community rallied to our side. The laptop program has become a point of pride as well as progress for Henrico County.

Get Parents Involved
Reach out to parents.
We work with parents to increase their capabilities and comfort level with the laptops. Our Parent Resource Centers offer train-

ing. At the high school level, parents can receive training in using the laptop, conducting research on the internet, and understanding the security features of the machine. One of the lasting advantages of this program is that it provides an educational resource for the entire family.

Our performance on the SOLs shows how technology can reinforce a commitment to rigorous content and high standards. At the same time, I believe our laptop program creates new possibilities for every student that go beyond what even the best test can measure. The one-on-one opportunity this program creates can become a defining feature of 21st-century schools.

THIRTEEN

Laptops for All Students Is Not Yet Practical

Bob Moore

In the following selection Bob Moore argues that school districts are too quick to adopt 1-to-1 computing (a term for programs that provide each student with a computer). Moore writes that such programs are too expensive and that few districts properly calculate the true cost to run them. He also notes the difficulty in finding and maintaining technological support for such ambitious programs. And he argues that the touted benefits of 1-to-1 computing, such as rising test scores, may be attributable to other factors. Moore is the executive director of information technology for the Blue Valley School District in Overland Park, Kansas.

In case you've been asleep for the past few years, there is a new vision for educational technology. This new vision—commonly known as 1-to-1 computing—is the latest in a long list for technology in K–12 schools, which over the years has included a computer lab in every school, computers in every classroom, a computer for every teacher, and all schools and classrooms connected to the internet.

In 1-to-1 computing, every student would have his or her own computer. Just like previous visions, this one makes perfect sense.

Bob Moore, "The 'Brutal Facts' of 1-to-1 Computing: Cost, Sustainability of 1-to-1 Programs Make Them Impractical – for Now," www.eSchoolNews.com, May 1, 2006. Copyright © 2007 eSchool News. All rights reserved. Reprinted with permission from eSchool News. For more information, please visit http://www.eschoolnews.com.

There will inevitably be a time when every student will have his or her own powerful, lightweight information and communication device—but now is not the time.

This conclusion about 1-to-1 computing is particularly troubling for me, given that I've had the good fortune to work in a school district for the past 11 years where the technology budget would be the envy of any school district across the nation. As I began to study the feasibility of 1-to-1 in my district, I came to the conclusion that even with our significant budget, we would have to give up investing in many high-impact technologies to be able to come close to affording and sustaining a district-wide 1-to-1 initiative. My conclusion ran counter to what was happening in states and districts across the country. They were buying into the 1-to-1 vision, tens of thousands of computers at a time. The more I studied the reports about these various initiatives, I was struck time and time again by the lack of clearly stated and measurable educational goals and the lack of consideration of total cost of ownership (TCO). Instead, proponents of 1-to-1 initiatives tend to rely on feel-good anecdotes and very soft data to stretch correlations with student achievement. Given that 1-to-1 initiatives are by far the most expensive we have ever pursued in K–12 technology, clearly we have a problem. . . .

You might be familiar with the Jim Collins leadership book *Good to Great*. One of my favorite concepts Collins discusses is what he refers to as "confronting the brutal facts." Some in the K–12 community might say that today's proponents of 1-to-1 are merely providing the necessary vision and leadership, but as Collins reminds us, "Yes, leadership is about vision. But leadership is equally about creating a climate where the truth is heard and the brutal facts confronted." As I see it, the brutal facts are those we chose to ignore because it might be uncomfortable or inconvenient should we acknowledge, let alone wrestle with, them.

It Is Not Affordable

In the spirit of Collins' *Good to Great*, let's confront the brutal facts about 1-to-1 computing in our schools. Brutal Fact One: In today's current hardware, software, and content markets, large-scale, long-term 1-to-1 initiatives are not affordable.

When I use the term *1-to-1*, I am referring to the practice of providing each student with his or her own powerful, full-featured notebook or tablet computer. Initiatives that rely on handheld computers or wireless notebook carts are not true 1-to-1 programs.

Even if a district can get a sweet deal on the computers and software, the costs of providing high-quality professional development, support, maintenance, and infrastructure will be prohibitive. When was the last time you heard representatives from any of the large 1-to-1 initiatives report on the program's complete, long-term TCO? Let me give you a hint: never, because they haven't calculated it—and if they did, they would find out the initiative is not sustainable. Fortunately, the Consortium for School Networking has begun examining the TCO of 1-to-1 initiatives in a few districts. When published, the results should be enlightening.

My concerns aside, there are a number of things that could dramatically change the market. The two that come to mind most quickly are open technologies and the work being done by Project Inkwell.

Open-source operating systems and applications are widely used in schools outside the U.S. We are just starting to see glimpses here of how they might dramatically change the economics of K–12 technology, thus lowering the cost of 1-to-1 significantly. The technical and functional requirements that Project Inkwell is developing for a true K–12 appropriate 1-to-1 device also might lead to a dramatic market shift—but it's unlikely that either of these factors will have any significant impact in the very near future.

It Is Difficult to Get Technical Support

Brutal Fact Two: Providing sufficient, high-quality professional development and technical support for even a modest K–12 technology initiative is difficult, particularly in these times of shrinking operations budgets. Considering the costs of these services for

Students work in a classroom at Philadelphia's School of the Future. The high school has laptops and workstations for all students but took three years, a partnership with Microsoft, and $63 million to create.

a 1-to-1 initiative is enough to give even a well-financed district technology leader a full-blown migraine.

We've all heard the stories of enlisting students in technical support and even in helping to train teachers. These stories have high feel-good quotients, but to suggest that you can rely largely on students for technical support is either naïve or irresponsible.

Any technology initiative needs to have a clear plan for professional development and technical support. Ideally, the professional development should be job-embedded and occur as part of an overall, systemic school improvement effort. As for technical support, 1-to-1 initiatives require districts to have experienced technical staff, particularly in the areas of mobile computing and wireless network infrastructure.

A recent visit of mine to a school in one of the nation's very large 1-to-1 initiatives illustrates the importance of technical support. A teacher who had been involved since the very beginning

Parents' Opinion of Laptops in Class

After two years, the first middle school children to use laptops in class showed no improvement in statewide MES tests, despite the state's heavy investment. Do you believe laptops will enhance your child's ability to learn?

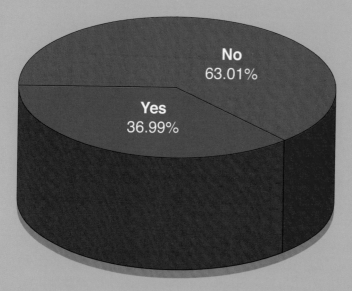

No
63.01%

Yes
36.99%

of the nearly four-year-long project told me that, because of inadequate technical support, he could not remember a day when every student in his class had his or her computer. If that is indeed a fact, it is truly brutal.

Reported Gains Might Not Be Due to Computers

Brutal Fact Three: The increases in student achievement that are being reported by some 1-to-1 initiatives might be merely convenient coincidences, rather than outcomes attributable to every student having his or her own computer. For the past several years, schools across the nation have been focusing on improving student achievement with unprecedented energy, thanks to the No Child Left Behind Act. Research tells us that when you implement curriculum aligned with standards, use formative and summative assessments aligned with this curriculum, and provide differentiated instruction to meet the needs of individual students' achievement, gains will follow. This is exactly what has been happening in schools today.

Granted, schools are still experiencing a range of success, but to attribute gains in student achievement solely to ubiquitous computing ignores the improvements we are seeing in curriculum, assessment, instruction, and professional development. Furthermore, specific, measurable gains in achievement are rarely identified as goals of 1-to-1 initiatives; rather, they are reported with a sigh of relief after the fact.

Benefits Do Not Stand Up to Close Examination

More Brutal Facts: Many of the other reported benefits of 1-to-1 do not necessarily stand up to close examination. Three of the most common are workforce preparedness (or learning 21st-century skills), student attendance, and parental involvement.

If workforce preparedness is a goal of 1-to-1 initiatives, why do the vast majority of initiatives start in the middle grades rather than in high school? Why are we ignoring students who could be entering the workforce in just a year or two? I have read all the reasons, but it still makes no sense. I think there are two overriding reasons. First, 1-to-1 would really shake up a high school—and not many school districts want to tackle true reform in the most sacred of education settings, the American comprehensive high school. Let's applaud the few that are trying. The second reason is that middle-level education is constantly under fire from a variety of directions. This atmosphere can give 1-to-1 initiatives cover in case of unmet expectations.

Students learning 21st-century skills is another common benefit cited of 1-to-1 initiatives. While these are critical, let's remember that most so-called 21st-century skills are really skills of the last two decades of the 20th century. Both Information Power (American Library Association, 1988) and the SCAN's Report (U.S. Department of Labor, 1991) provide the foundation for the 21st-century skills so often referenced today.

Neither suggests 1-to-1 computer initiatives, nor will 1-to-1 magically prepare students with 21st-century skills.

It would be impossible to argue the importance of student attendance and parental involvement on achievement. While 1-to-1 initiatives might temporarily have an effect on both, these initiatives will not solve the deeply entrenched cultural and economic factors that can affect parental involvement and student attendance. When I came into this profession nearly two decades ago, the school district I worked for at that time had just installed ILS (integrated learning system) computer labs in each of its elementary schools. I clearly remember that increased parental involvement and student achievement were stated benefits of these outrageously expensive labs.

Technology in the Classroom Is Inevitable
But there is hope. . . .

Jim Collins in *Good to Great* tells us to "confront the brutal facts, yet never lose faith." The new vision for 1-to-1 computing in our schools inevitably will come to pass. It is part of the natural evolution of educational technology. To achieve this vision, however, we must be thoughtful and deliberate in our actions. We must have (brutally) honest dialog about the challenges. We need to have clear, measurable achievement goals. For our classroom teachers, we need to provide ongoing, job-embedded professional development. Reliable technical support must be provided. It also is critical that we come to understand the true TCO of long-term, large-scale initiatives so we can budget appropriately. With these in place, we can begin to assess and communicate the true value of 1-1, so we can avoid falling victim to the false promise of the past—and ultimately are successful in our vision.

FOURTEEN

Students with Laptops Are Less Engaged in Class

David Cole

In the following selection David Cole, a professor at Georgetown University Law Center, explains why he has banned computers from his class, even though all incoming students at Georgetown are required to have computers. He notes that students who have laptops spend too much time on extensive note-taking. This, he argues, puts their focus on the note-taking and not on the actual issues that are being discussed. He also has found that students get distracted by various computer temptations such as surfing the Web, checking e-mail, or sending instant messages to friends.

"Could you repeat the question?"

In recent years, that has become the most common response to questions I pose to my law students at Georgetown University. It is usually asked while the student glances up from the laptop screen that otherwise occupies his or her field of vision. After I repeat the question, the student's gaze as often as not returns to the computer screen, as if the answer might magically appear there. Who knows, with instant messaging, maybe it will.

Some years back, our law school, like many around the country, wired its classrooms with Internet hookups. It's the way of the future, I was told. Now we are a wireless campus, and incoming students are required to have laptops. So my first-year students were a bit surprised when I announced at the first class this year that laptops were banned from my classroom.

College students work on their laptops during a class. Some argue that laptops can make students less engaged in the classroom experience.

Using Computers for Class

Have you participated in the following activities this year as part of a Stanford course?

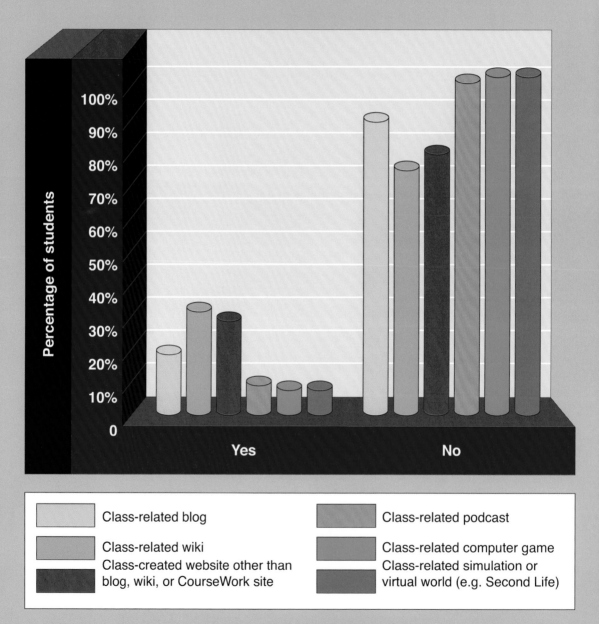

Class-related blog		Class-related podcast
Class-related wiki		Class-related computer game
Class-created website other than blog, wiki, or CourseWork site		Class-related simulation or virtual world (e.g. Second Life)

I did this for two reasons, I explained. Note-taking on a laptop encourages verbatim transcription. The note-taker tends to go into stenographic mode and no longer processes information in a way that is conducive to the give and take of classroom discussion. Because taking notes the old-fashioned way, by hand, is so much slower, one actually has to listen, think and prioritize the most important themes.

Too Many Temptations

In addition, laptops create temptation to surf the Web, check e-mail, shop for shoes or instant-message friends. That's not only distracting to the student who is checking Red Sox statistics but for all those who see him, and many others, doing something besides being involved in class. Together, the stenographic mode and Web surfing make for a much less engaged classroom, and that affects all students (not to mention me).

I agreed to permit two volunteers to use laptops to take notes that would be made available to all students. And that first day I allowed everyone to use the laptops they had with them. I posed a question, and a student volunteered an answer. I answered her with a follow-up question. As if on cue, as soon as I started to respond, the student went back to typing—and then asked, "Could you repeat the question?"

When I have raised with my colleagues the idea of cutting off laptop access, some accuse me of being paternalistic, authoritarian or worse. We daydreamed and did crosswords when we were students, they argue, so how can we prohibit our students, who are adults after all, from using their time in class as they deem fit?

A crossword hidden under a book is one thing. With the aid of Microsoft and Google, we have effectively put at every seat a library of magazines, a television and the opportunity for real-time side conversations and invited our students to check out whenever they find their attention wandering.

I feel especially strongly about this issue because I'm addicted to the Internet myself. I checked my e-mail at least a dozen times while writing this op-ed. I've often resolved, after a rare and liberating weekend away from e-mail, that I will wait till the end of the day to read e-mail at the office. Yet, almost as if it is beyond my control, e-mail is the first thing I check when I log on each morning. As for multitasking, I don't buy it. Attention diverted is attention diverted.

A Laptop-Free Classroom Works

But this is all theory. How does banning laptops work in practice? My own sense has been that my class is much more engaged than recent past classes. I'm biased, I know. So I conducted an anonymous survey of my students after about six weeks—by computer, of course.

The results were striking. About 80 percent reported that they are more engaged in class discussion when they are laptop-free. Seventy percent said that, on balance, they liked the no-laptop policy. And perhaps most surprising, 95 percent admitted that they use their laptops in class for "purposes other than taking notes, such as surfing the Web, checking e-mail, instant messaging and the like." Ninety-eight percent reported seeing fellow students do the same.

I am sure that the Internet can be a useful pedagogical tool in some settings and for some subjects. But for most classes, it is little more than an attractive nuisance. Technology has outstripped us on this one, and we need to reassess its appropriate and inappropriate role in teaching. The personal computer has revolutionized our lives, in many ways for the better. But it also threatens to take over our lives. At least for some purposes, unplugging may still be the best response.

FIFTEEN

PDAs Can Be Useful in the Classroom

Diane Curtis

The following article details the positives of handheld computers, or PDAs, in the classroom. Diane Curtis writes about classrooms in which PDAs are not only allowed but are part of the curriculum. She notes that students think they are fun to use: students can "beam" information to each other, can use them in classes ranging from science to gym. "A routine classroom task becomes a novelty because students can animate pictures that accompany their written reports," writes Curtis. "Flash cards become a fun computer game." Curtis is a veteran educational writer and former editor for the George Lucas Education Foundation.

Handheld computers, the wallet-sized organizational devices used by business professionals to keep track of appointments, contacts, e-mail, and the Internet, have found their way into classrooms.

Students do science experiments outdoors with computerized probes and watch graphs come alive on the spot as they enter spreadsheet data. Teachers eliminate the need to write assignments on the blackboard because they can "beam" instructions to students' handhelds. A routine classroom task becomes a novelty because students can animate pictures that accompany their written reports. Flash cards become a fun computer game.

"For once, I think education is keeping up with what's going on in the real world and not sitting there chiseling something into a rock," says science teacher Laurie Ritchey, whose district in suburban Chicago was ahead of the pack in outfitting its students and teachers with the computers, also known as personal digital assistants or PDAs.

In one of the first large-scale school implementations, Consolidated High School District 230 in Orland Park, Illinois, equipped its three high schools with 2,200 Palm IIIxe's in the fall of 2000 in the form of both classroom sets and individual handhelds that could be bought or rented by students.

Affordability, Portability, Versatility

Darrell Walery, district director of technology, cites affordability, portability, and versatility as the reasons he believes the tiny computers will grow in popularity with educators. "The economic factor is a really important piece of the puzzle. I can't buy a laptop for every kid, but I may be able to buy a handheld for every kid," he says. In one year, the cost of the handhelds dropped from $225 to $100. The fact that the PDA is so versatile it can be used in P.E. classes to determine whether a student is fit, on field trips to take oxygen readings, or in art classes to make animated drawings points to its advantages. But the biggest plus, Walery believes, is that students have access to the digital devices 24 hours a day. They don't have to wait to get on the computer in a lab or in class. The information and applications they need are always at their fingertips.

There may even be a more important advantage, claim Ritchey and other teachers.

"What you rope is kids' enthusiasm," says Ritchey, who teaches at Carl Sandburg High School. "Paper and pencil works fine, but this is kind of a cooler way of doing it."

"I guess the best thing about the Palm Pilot is (students) like it so much," echoes Janet Manning, a special education teacher at nearby Stagg High School. The fun students have with the PDAs masks the seriousness of the effort, adds Stagg geography teacher Josh Barron. "I think they don't even realize they're learning."

Round-Robin Beaming

Barron and his students often go through the strange-looking rite of "beaming" information to each other. With PDA in the palm of his hand, Barron will point his handheld at a student's and tap the word "beam" on the screen menu. That student will then do the same with another student until all the handhelds have had infrared ray contact.

Ritchey's class used the handhelds for an assignment to create an ecological footprint, a measurement of the human impact on

Sixth-grade students at Ridgeway Elementary in Olanthe, Kansas, use Palm Pilot PDAs to complete a class assignment.

nature in terms of the land and water used for human consumption and waste. The assignment started with Ritchey beaming worksheet questions, which she was easily able to modify for the next classes when questions came up. The students' job was to record more than 100 facts on their handhelds, such as how much the students' families ate, how much energy they used, how much their laundry weighed, how much garbage they generated, and the square footage of their homes.

Rather than transfer written answers to a computer, the students were able to input the data at their homes. When the students returned to school, they logged onto the Ecological Footprint Web site, and transferred the information into the school computer through a method of communication called synchronization or hot sync. The Web site then translated the student data into number of hectares of land that they used to live. What many students discovered was that they were using five or more hectares of earth. The Web site estimates that 2.2 hectares is the amount that can accommodate human needs without damaging the earth.

For another assignment, the students attached a probe, a special sensing device, to the PDAs and took them outside to measure oxygen concentrations in a pond. Probes were dropped into various areas and depths of water to measure the effect of sunlight on plant growth. That information was instantly graphed using special software. Students were able to test a variable and instantly see a live, moving graph illustrating their results in real time as opposed to the more familiar method of obtaining data and graphing it hours later. "The instantaneous generation of information," says Ritchey, "leads to more accurate conclusions during the lab process."

Variety of Uses

Use of the handhelds has not been confined to science classes. English teacher Jean Lombaer used the handhelds with a class of sophomores reading below grade level and witnessed noticeable improvements in their work. Her students used a flash card pro-

Teacher Evaluation of Handheld Computers by Subject

Having a classroom set of handhelds will improve the quality of the learning activities I can implement with my students.

Subject	Disagree/Strongly Disagree	Neither Agree or Disagree	Agree/Strongly Agree
Chemistry			100%
Physics			100%
Environmental Science	3.7%		96.3%
Science	5.7%		94.3%
Biology	5.9%		94.2%
Technology or Engineering	6.3%		93.8%
English	7.7%	7.7%	84.7%
Math	3.8%	15.4%	80.8%
English Language Learning		20%	80.0%
Reading Language	4.3%	21.7%	73.9%
Social Studies	9.5%	19%	71.4%
Physical Education		33.3%	66.7%

0% 10% 20% 30% 40% 50% 60% 70% 80% 90% 100%

Legend: Disagree/Strongly Disagree | Neither Agree or Disagree | Agree/Strongly Agree

Taken from: SRI International

gram to enter vocabulary words and definitions and track right and wrong answers.

"I'm not going to tell you that it's because the Palm is better than flash cards, but it's brand new for the kids, and the delight of working with new technology caused them to learn a lot of the things I wanted them to learn," she says. As another aid to memorizing vocabulary, her students used a software program to draw a picture to accompany the words. The picture can be animated.

Handhelds encourage greater peer editing, Lombaer adds, noting that students can easily transfer draft copies of papers to each other and make revisions using inexpensive keyboards. Her students are more willing to revise when they can type in words rather than having to write by hand. If tapping in letters with a stylus were the only option, she says, the tiny computers would not be nearly as useful. She also used the PDAs for tests, revamping the format so that students worked in small groups and "beaming" answers among students was an asset rather than an "F."

Kim Onak, a Stagg biology teacher who keeps a set of handhelds for her special education class, says the assignment and project planner capabilities of the computers—their original functions—should not be underestimated. Her students are much more organized with the PDAs and use them to, among other things, keep track of grades and assignments.

Here to Stay

The kids agree.

"It's very useful in writing things down. Before, you'd have to keep everything in paper, and things would get lost."

"It's so much easier to take notes."

"It's fun."

"You don't have to worry about losing your spiral. Then, there're always the games."

Ritchey, the Sandburg High biology teacher, notes that uses continue to multiply. "We're definitely on an evolutionary trail," she says.

SIXTEEN

Electronic Devices Enable Bullying

Editorial Board of the *Portsmouth Herald*

> The editorial board at the *Portsmouth Herald* in Washington
> State wrote the following piece to alert parents, school
> administrators, and communities about the dangers of cyber-
> bullying. Cyber-bullying, which is someone using technol-
> ogy to bully someone else, has become increasingly com-
> mon among students. With technology, the piece reads,
> bullies can now "unleash putdowns, nasty rumors, [and]
> humiliating pictures in e-mails, blogs and chat rooms." To
> solve the problem, the editorial board offers several recom-
> mendations. Among them are making children, teachers,
> and schools aware of the problem and supporting laws that
> help schools to stop cyber-bullying.

The *Portsmouth Herald* Editorial Board would like to raise
awareness of a new and rapidly expanding type of bullying
that is hurting our children—cyber-bullying.

The evolving age of the Internet and emerging electronic technologies is dramatically impacting the social lives of our children.
The ABC's of safely navigating the Web, promoted by law enforcement's I-safe program, helps our children to circumnavigate unde-
sirable Web sites. Yet many of our kids are oblivious to the dangers

"Internet Age Brings New Form of Harassment: Cyber-Bullying," *The Portsmouth Herald*, March
30, 2005. Copyright © 2005 Seacoast Media Group. Reproduced by permission.

Students and Cyber-Bullying

Nearly 90 percent of children reported being bullied and 59 percent said they had bullied other students.

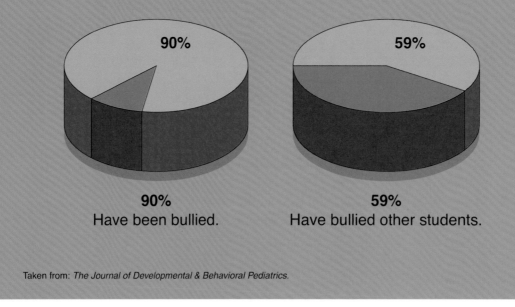

90%
Have been bullied.

59%
Have bullied other students.

Taken from: *The Journal of Developmental & Behavioral Pediatrics.*

of cyber-bullies and sexual predators as they disclose personal information, names, addresses and work locations freely on blogs and in chat rooms. The FBI notes that many kids will not talk to strangers but will say anything on the Internet.

Cyber-Bullying in School

Bullying in our schools: Our local police work actively with our schools using the Kids and Company program to educate our children about the dangerous and destructive impact of bullying. Unlike teasing, where a child may feel uncomfortable but able to handle the situation on their own, bullying requires an adult to step in. Bullying must be taken seriously and may do long-term emotional damage. Do not think it is a normal part of childhood.

Federal statistics claim approximately 30 percent of teens in the United States (over 5.7 million) are involved in bullying, either as the bully or as the target. Bullying leads our children to feel tense, anxious and afraid. It impacts concentration in school, self-esteem and feelings of self-worth, it increases social isolation and may lead to depression and avoidance of attending school. Raising awareness by increasing teacher, parent and principal supervision, as well as forming and enforcing clear rules and strong social norms against bullying, provides support and protection for all our kids.

While bullying usually occurs in our schools and on buses going home, we all need a wake-up call to focus on emerging cyber-bullying. Few of us know anything about this. Wiredkids.org, an organization monitoring children's use of the Internet, claims that the emergence of cyber-bullying has intensified teen angst. It allows bullies to unleash putdowns; nasty rumors; humiliating pictures in e-mails, blogs and chat rooms; and verbal and physical threats that can strike victims at home and at any time. Many other children anonymously participate or are witness to this.

The damage can be devastating. Cyber bullies, mostly ages 9–14, use anonymity on the Web to dish out pain without witnessing consequences aggravated by use of cell phones. Wiredkids.org surveyed 3,000 children in the last six months. Half said they were either bullied, were guilty of cyber-bullying, or knew someone who was bullied. Kids may not tell their parents what is going on out of fear of being banned from using the Internet.

Schools Have to "Walk a Fine Line"

Cyber-bullying requires school officials to walk a fine line to protect children who are bullied without trampling on the free speech rights of the alleged bullies. Schools may risk litigation from parents if they take action. On the other hand, what can a parent do if someone is destroying their child's reputation in chat rooms on the Internet?

This is what we can do as individuals and as a community. Explore with your child, teacher and school to identify if your child is aware of and witness to cyber-bullying. Find out what chat rooms they log on to. Explore resources for parents. Look at SammySnail.com, the Web site that recently won (out of a juried pool of 200) the New Hampshire Award for best Internet site

John Halligan displays a Web page devoted to his son, Ryan. Ryan committed suicide in 2003, an act his father blames on months of cyber-bullying.

based on quality and content addressing bullying and conflict resolution. This Web site will link you to numerous resources. Look into WireSafety.org and Teenangels.org to see how our teens in the Seacoast can be empowered to reverse the evolving cyber-bullying trend.

School boards, administrators, and local and state government need to pay attention to this new and negative use of the Internet. New Hampshire needs to look at legislation in the Washington State Senate. This month [March 2005] they're voting on SB5849, which amends language in current state law on bullying to include electronic means of communication via e-mails, Internet-based communications, pager service, cell phones and electronic text messaging. This will give legal recourse for our parents and schools to protect our children from cyber-bullies.

In the new age of Internet resources at our fingertips, we must be vigilant of those abusive and destructive end users, cyber-bullies that now prey on our children. We all need to better educate ourselves on this issue.

What You Should Know About Electronic Devices in Schools

Facts About Electronic Device Bans

- Calculators were some of the first electronic devices to be banned from classrooms. (Ironically, now calculators are often required in class.)
- In the 1980s schools banned pagers, alleging a connection between pagers and gangs and drugs.
- New York City schools have some of the country's strictest bans on electronic devices. New York City schools have banned wireless devices from school since the 1980s, but Mayor Michael Bloomberg started aggressively enforcing the ban in 2006 by subjecting students to random searches with metal detectors.
- In Detroit schools cell phones are banned, in Boston they are allowed to be carried out of sight, and in Los Angeles they can only be used between classes.

Facts About Cell Phones at School

- Nearly a third of teenagers in the United States carry a cell phone.
- Many parents became advocates of cell phones at school after learning that students at the Columbine shootings were able to call their parents during the shooting to report their whereabouts.

- Sixty-eight percent of school-based security officers believe that student use of cell phones would detract from school safety in a crisis. Cell phone use during an emergency could create confusion, jam local phone networks, and hamper rumor control.
- Some proposed plans to thwart school cell phone use include radio devices that detect cell phone signals, jamming cell phone signals, and classroom paint that blocks calls.
- Some student tactics to thwart cell phone bans include hiding the gadgets inside sandwich rolls and stashing them at local stores for a small holding fee.

Other Electronic Devices

- An estimated 7 percent of school districts provide some students with handheld computers or PDAs.
- In 2004 college freshmen spent an average of $1,176.82 on electronic devices.
- In a 2007 Canadian study, college students with computers reported doing the following non-school-related tasks in class: 81 percent checked e-mail, 68 percent used instant messaging, 43 percent surfed the Internet, and 25 percent played games.
- Though advocates of MP3 players in school point to their use as a study tool, most students (85 percent) use them for listening to music, 10 percent use them for video, and 5 percent use them for listening to podcasts or audiobooks.
- Seventy percent of YouTube's registered users are American, and about 50 percent of these are under twenty years of age.
- In 2006 a *Wall Street Journal* report calculated that in one year the people of the world had watched 9,305 years' worth of videos.
- In a 2005 British study 20 percent of students had experienced some sort of cyber-bullying.
- Electronic devices can aid cheating in many ways: Students can use cell phones and PDAs to text each other answers,

iPods can be used as virtual crib sheets, wired students can look up answers on the Internet, and cameras can be used to take pictures of exams.

- Increasingly, prospective college students are choosing schools based on technological factors. About 80 percent of colleges had wireless networks covering at least part of their campuses in 2004, up from 30 percent in 2000.
- In 2004, Duke University gave each of its incoming freshman a free iPod. In 2005, 75 percent of Duke freshmen reported using the iPods for academic work.
- Ninety-eight percent of K–12 schools have Internet access.

What You Should Do About Electronic Devices in Schools

After studying the issues and discovering what you believe, you can take action in many ways. Find out what your school's policy is and the reasons it was put into place. If you disagree with the policy, you can write a piece for your school paper explaining why you think the rule should be changed. You can also arrange to speak at a local PTA meeting and explain clearly and calmly how the rule could be changed. Enlisting adults to your cause can help.

Local newspapers are also a good source for publicity. You can write a piece for the editorial page or call the paper and try to interest a reporter in covering the topic. You are more likely to get the reporter to write an article on your story if you can provide them with a reason that it is a topic of local interest.

Check the list of organizations listed in the back of this book and also on the Internet to find an existing group that already has experience in these kinds of issues. Existing groups have information on legal precedents and can provide you with advice or support. Peacefire, for example, is an organization that provides information on legal issues about students, freedom of speech, and Internet access.

Whichever position you take, plenty of research and evidence exists to promote your point of view. For example, you can find plenty of commentary stating that cell phones do not help in emergencies and just as much stating the opposite. If you think that electronic devices should be allowed, you can research cases in which schools have embraced technology and had successful results. If you think electronic devices should be banned, you can cite cases of cheating or of students not paying attention in class.

Whichever point of view you take, it is likely that you will have to continually adjust your opinion as new electronic devices are invented that are smaller, faster, and have capabilities that we cannot yet even dream of.

ORGANIZATIONS TO CONTACT

The editors have compiled the following list of organizations con-
cerned with the issues debated in this book. The descriptions are
derived from materials provided by the organizations. All have
publications or information available for interested readers. The
list was compiled on the date of publication of the present volume; the information provided here may change. Be aware that
many organizations take several weeks or longer to respond to
inquiries, so allow as much time as possible.

Association for the Advancement of Computing in Education (AACE)
PO Box 1545, Chesapeake, VA 23327-1545
(757) 366-5606
e-mail: info@aace.org
Web site: www.aace.org

The AACE is an international educational and professional not-
for-profit organization dedicated to the advancement of the knowledge, theory, and quality of learning and teaching at all levels with
information technology. The purpose of AACE is accomplished
through the encouragement of scholarly inquiry related to information technology in education and the dissemination of research
results and their applications through publications, conferences,
societies and chapters, and interorganizational projects.

Center for Children & Technology (CCT)
96 Morton St., 7th Fl., New York, NY 10014
(212) 807-4200
e-mail: sp@edc.org
Web site: www.cct.edc.org

CCT investigates ways that technology can make a difference in
children's classrooms, schools, and communities through a num-

ber of basic, applied, formative, and summative research projects. Its goal is to construct a more complete understanding of how to foster greater equity, student achievement, and teacher preparedness in our nation's schools. The center's research often is situated within classrooms and schools because context is of vital importance to any educational intervention.

The Consortium for School Networking (CoSN)
1025 Vermont Ave. NW, Suite 1010, Washington, DC 20005
(202) 861-2676
e-mail: info@cosn.org
Web site: www.cosn.org

CoSN is a voice for K–12 education leaders who use technology strategically to improve teaching and learning. CoSN provides products and services to support leadership development, advocacy, coalition building, and awareness of emerging technologies.

First Amendment Schools
1703 N. Beauregard St., Alexandria, VA 22311-1714
(800) 933-2723
e-mail: mmccloskey@ascd.org
Web site: www.firstamendmentschools.org

First Amendment Schools: Educating for Freedom and Responsibility is a national reform initiative designed to transform how schools teach and practice the rights and responsibilities of citizenship that frame civic life in our democracy. To achieve its mission, the First Amendment Schools project has four primary goals: to create consensus guidelines and guiding principles for all schools interested in creating and sustaining First Amendment principles in their school; to establish schools in every region of the nation where First Amendment principles are understood and applied throughout the school community; to encourage and develop curriculum reforms that reinvigorate and deepen teaching about the First Amendment across the curriculum; and to educate school leaders, teachers, school board members, attorneys, and other key stakeholders about the meaning and significance of First Amendment principles and ideals.

The George Lucas Educational Foundation (GLEF)
PO Box 3494, San Rafael, CA 94912
(415) 662-1600
e-mail: edutopia@glef.org
Web site: www.edutopia.org

The George Lucas Educational Foundation was founded in 1991 as a nonprofit operating foundation to celebrate and encourage innovation in schools. GLEF documents, disseminates, and advocates for exemplary programs in K–12 public schools to help these practices spread nationwide. It publishes the stories of innovative teaching and learning through a variety of media—a magazine, e-newsletters, DVDs, books, and its Web site.

International Society for Technology in Education (ISTE)
1710 Rhode Island Ave. NW, Suite 900, Washington, DC 20036
(866) 654-4777
e-mail: iste@iste.org
Web site: www.iste.org

The International Society for Technology in Education is a source for professional development, knowledge generation, advocacy, and leadership for innovation. A nonprofit membership organization, ISTE provides leadership and service to improve teaching, learning, and school leadership by advancing the effective use of technology in pre-K–12 and teacher education. Home of the National Educational Technology Standards (NETS), the Center for Applied Research in Educational Technology (CARET), and the National Educational Computing Conference (NECC), ISTE represents more than eighty-five thousand professionals worldwide.

National Coalition Against Censorship (NCAC)
275 Seventh Ave., Suite 1504, New York, NY 10001
(212) 807-6222

e-mail: ncac@ncac.org
Web site: www.ncac.org

The National Coalition Against Censorship, founded in 1974, is an alliance of fifty national nonprofit organizations, including literary, artistic, religious, educational, professional, labor, and civil liberties groups. United by a conviction that freedom of thought, inquiry, and expression must be defended, they work to educate their members and the public at large about the dangers of censorship and how to oppose them.

National School Boards Association (NSBA)
1680 Duke St., Alexandria, VA 22314
(703) 838-6722
e-mail: info@nsba.org
Web site: www.nsba.org

The National School Boards Association established the Institute for the Transfer of Technology to Education (ITTE) in 1985 with its federation of state school boards associations. The mission of ITTE: Education Technology Programs advances NSBA's shared strategic vision that states, "Every school board will lead its community in preparing all students to succeed in a rapidly changing global society." ITTE is committed to engaging education, industry, and policy leaders to improve education processes and outcomes through knowledge and understanding of technology and organizational development. ITTE continues to serve the many constituencies of NSBA through its involvement in national advocacy efforts, research, publications, meetings, and its school district membership program, the Technology Leadership Network.

Peacefire
14615 NE Thirtieth Pl., Suite 10D, Bellevue, WA 98007
(425) 497-9002
e-mail: bennett@peacefire.org
Web site: www.peacefire.org

Peacefire was created in August 1996 to represent the interests of people under eighteen in the debate over freedom of speech on the Internet. Peacefire is a "people for young people's freedom of speech" organization, not a "young people for freedom of speech" organization. In other words, people of any age can join if they are against censorship for students and people under eighteen in general. Peacefire provides facts and research for use by larger organizations in legal battles.

Technology Student Association
1914 Association Dr., Reston, VA 20191-1540
(703) 860-9000
e-mail: general@tsaweb.org
Web site: www.tsaweb.org

The mission of the Technology Student Association is to prepare its membership for the challenges of a dynamic world by promoting technological literacy, leadership, and problem-solving skills, resulting in personal growth and opportunities.

Books

Larry Cuban, *Oversold and Underused: Computers in the Classroom.* Boston: Harvard University Press, 2003.

The George Lucas Education Foundation, *Edutopia: Success Stories for Learning in the Digital Age.* San Francisco: Jossey-Bass, 2002.

Gerard Goggin, *Cell Phone Culture: Mobile Technology in Everyday Life.* New York: Routledge, 2006.

Todd Oppenheimer, *The Flickering Mind: Saving Education from the False Promise of Technology.* New York: Random House, 2004.

Will Richardson, *Blogs, Wikis, Podcasts and Other Powerful WebTools for Classrooms.* Thousand Oaks, CA: Corwin, 2006.

Carolyn Staudt, *Changing How We Teach and Learn with Handheld Computers.* Thousand Oaks, CA: Corwin, 2004.

Bard Williams, *Handheld Computers and Smartphones in Secondary Schools: A Guide to Hands-on Learning.* Eugene, OR: International Society for Technology in Education, 2006.

Periodicals

Elisa Batista, "Debating Merits of Palms in Class," *Wired*, August 23, 2001.

Jacqueline Hicks Grazette, "Can Teachers Keep Up with the iPod Generation?" *Dallas Morning News*, April 15, 2007.

L.A. Johnson, "Growing Use of Camera Cell Phones Shows How New Technology Can Bring Out the Best and the Worst," *Pittsburgh Post-Gazette*, October 27, 2004.

Elizabeth Armstrong Moore, "When iPod Goes Collegiate," *Christian Science Monitor*, April 19, 2005. www.csmonitor.com/2005/0419/p11s01-legn.html.

Mary Niederberger, "Technology: Boon or Bane? Cell Phones, PDAs Spur Debate in Schools," *Pittsburgh Post-Gazette*, December 1, 2004.

Sherry Parmet, "It's Hard to Make the Call on Cell Phones," *San Diego Union-Tribune*, January 1, 2005.

Maia Ridberg, "Professors Want Their Classes 'Unwired,'" *Christian Science Monitor*, May 4, 2006.

Carolyn Said, "Are Camera Phones Too Revealing?" *San Francisco Chronicle*, May 16, 2004.

Internet Sources

Cara Branigan, "Camera Phones Call Up Privacy Fears for Schools," *eSchool News Online*, January 12, 2004. www.eschool news.com/news/showstory.cfm?ArticleID=4835.

Jenna Lo Castro, "Text Messaging in Class," *CarrollNewsOnline*, March 6, 2006. www.carrollnewsonline.com/index.php?id=359.

Michael Geist, "We're All on Candid Camera," *Michael Geist*, November 27, 2006. www.michaelgeist.ca/content/view/ 1551/159.

Lee Gomes, "Will All of Us Get Our 15 Minutes on a YouTube Video?" *Wall Street Journal Online*, August 30, 2006. http://online. wsj.com/public/article/58115689298168048904- wWyrSwyn6RfV fz9NwLk774VUWc_200770829.html?mod=rss_free.

Stephen Hutcheon, "YouTube Bans Don't Work," *Sydney Morning Herald*, March 8, 2007. www.smh.com.au/news/web/why-you tube-bans-dont-work/2007/03/08/1173166844770.html?s_ cid=rss_technology.

Elizabeth Melville, "Cell Phones: Nuisance or Necessity?" *Teaching Today*, April 2006. www.glencoe.com/sec/teachingtoday/edu cationupclose.phtml/52.

Madlen Read, "Growing Numbers of Students Use MP3 Players as a Study Tool," *Napa Valley Register*, February 7, 2007. www.napa valleyregister.com/articles/2007/02/07/business/local/doc45 c9e13a31a447296818650.txt.

Mark Rockwell, "How Smart Are School Phone Bans?" *Wireless Week*, June 15, 2006. www.wirelessweek.com/article.axpx ?id=71008.

Sarah Schmidt, "Study Finds Laptops in Class Hinder Learning," *Canada.com*, February 1, 2007. www.canada.com/topics/tech nology/story.html?id=9cb704c8-6f20-4276-ae5c-458a40ebS fbb&k=46022.

Sadhana Smiles, "Bullying Shifts from Playground to Cyberspace," *Age*, April 1, 2005. www.theage.com.au/news/Opinion/Bullying-shifts-from-playground-to-cyberspace/2005/03/31/111186 2526840.html.

Amy Standen, "My Friend Flickr," *Edutopia*, March 12, 2007. www.edutopia.org/my-friend-flickr.

INDEX